JIM NEAT

For his great grandchildren
Lena, Becca, Tommy and Peter

JIM NEAT

*The Case of a Young Man
Down on His Luck*

Mary J. Oliver

SEREN

Seren is the book imprint of
Poetry Wales Press Ltd
57 Nolton Street, Bridgend, Wales, CF31 3AE
www.serenbooks.com
Facebook: facebook.com/SerenBooks
Twitter: @SerenBooks

ISBN: 978-178-172-514-6

A CIP record for this title is available from the British Library.

The publisher acknowledges the financial assistance of the Welsh Books Council.

Cover: Southampton City Archives, Received Set, Britain, Merchant Seamen, 1921.

Printed by Latimer Trend & Company, Plymouth.

Contents

TORONTO GAOL

CORRESPONDENCE
to refer to family matters only

PARCELS
containing tobacco and food prohibited

MAGAZINES/BOOKS
with gun stories strictly forbidden

VISITS AND LETTERS
Remanded inmates: two visits/two letters weekly
Sentenced inmates: one visit/one letter weekly

VISITING HOURS
Daily except Saturday, Sunday and Holidays:
From 9.30 – 11 a.m.

INMATE'S LETTER TO BE WRITTEN ON REVERSE

Nov 19th 1935

Dearest Baby Queen

I'm sorry, but this is where I am. I've committed no felony but have gone to the dogs. Lizbietta is dead. I can hardly remember what's happened since then. I ended up in Toronto, taking narcotics again. You can imagine the results. I've been and still am going through absolute hell, in and out of this place more times than I can count.

It will be hard for you to understand how tough a place this country can be. Please keep this from Dad. Outside of that, I need no help.

Your loving brother

Jim

INMATE

WHITBY HOSPITAL, ONTARIO
CASE-NOTES

Admission of:
James William Spencer Neat, known as Jim

Date: Saturday 23rd November 1935, 5.25 pm

Age: 31

Address: Vagrant

Place/Date of Birth: Penge, England, 1904

Condition on arrival:
Comatose. Skin bluish, moist. Breathing depressed. Temperature 94.8 F

Diagnosis:
Heroin/opium overdose / addiction?
Suspected suicide attempt?
Duodenal / peptic ulcer?

Prescribed Treatment:
Hot bath. Physical rest. Neutralization of acid. Regular meals. Bland food. Licorice sweets. Camomile tea.

Comments:
Patient seriously unkempt. Would appear to have been homeless for many months. Rousable 2 hours after admission but unwilling to discuss circumstances. Appears to be in a state of physical and spiritual breakdown. Keep on Admissions Ward for observation.

Admitting Officer:
D. Fletcher, M.D. Superintendent

Saturday 30th November 1935

Since Mr Neat was admitted a week ago he has been withdrawn and at some risk to himself. I feel strongly that he should not be given insulin shock treatment. In my opinion he has suffered severe trauma and until we discover what that was I have no intention of treating him as insane. He is to be prescribed conservatively with warm baths, good food, a peaceful environment and the opportunity to talk.

The discomfort of his overdose/withdrawal is now passing and I am optimistic that we will soon learn more.

D. Fletcher

Monday 2nd December 1935

I have arranged for Jim Neat to be moved to Cottage 11, in the hope that the view of the lake from his bed and the proximity of the garden will restore his interest in living.

That our distinguished patient Professor Schofield resides there will be advantageous to them both. Frank suffered a severe breakdown, was forced to take sick leave from the Ontario Veterinary College, where he is Professor of Bacteriology, to recuperate away from both work and family. When first admitted six months ago, he talked at length to me about his loss of faith, and about his son, whom he raised alone after his wife died. He felt that he had not been a good father; that he had been too wedded to his work. Since the son left home last year to attend university in Toronto, he has cut off all contact with his father. Easy to understand how this brought about a total spiritual collapse in Frank.

Although I do not yet know what reduced Jim to his parlous state, I am confident the two will get on.

D. Fletcher

Monday 9th December 1935

He agreed to attend Mrs MacTaggart's writing class, but on the first occasion covered his sheet of paper with blasphemous obscenities. He returned the next day to apologise, overcome with embarrassment. Mrs MacTaggart told him he would get one more chance.

She then encouraged him to write in the present tense, to use a free, creative form, including imaginary postcards he might have sent home, revealing difficulties he faced on arrival in Canada.

(See attached papers).

D. Fletcher

A Squirrel Scorched

Canada, April 1926

I lie on my bunk in the detention centre, over-hear a conversation.

'Did you hear about the squirrel that scorched itself on a power cable? Set fire to the stables of the Winnipeg Race Track? Eleven thoroughbreds stampeded into The Red River and froze to death. Their heads are still sticking out the ice, like tombstones. And now teenage lovers are having sex for all to see between the blackened skulls, their frosted britches draped over handy jawbones. Didn't you hear about it?'

I curse this country where I'd hoped to find work and a wife — and dream of her.

Signed Jim Neat

Imaginary Widow

Lumber Camp, North Saskatchewan, December, 1926

Electro-chainsaws
arrived last week
from Germany.
'Job'll be kids' stuff now'
boss said.
A lie.
My mate was killed
the first day –
a dead branch

fell
out of the tree
he was ripping into.
Widow-makers they're called.
How I long
for the woman
who'll be widowed
if one falls
on me.

Signed Jim Neat

Unsent Postcards

1926

February, a North Saskatchewan lumber-camp, Dearest Baby Queen, Temperature dropped by 20 degrees in two hours. Boss says, 'Bring the horses in, their eyeballs freeze at 40.' Too late. We drag six blind cart-horses into the bunkhouse; lucky bastards, get fed and blanketed damned sight better than we do. Driven out by the stink of their shit. Your ever-loving brother, Jim

1926

August, Alberta, Dearest Baby Queen, Eking out a living weeding dandelions from between slabs on the sidewalks. With no place to hide from the sun, wind or dust, I see red, use the knife meant for hoicking out tap roots for something else. Your ever-loving brother, Jim

1927

December, Prince Albert Jail. Shovelling snow from one end of the compound to the other. When I've finished, I have to sweep it back again. Three thousand inmates here, they say. Ropes slung across corridors are for us to hang over after dark. Both index fingers gone. Don't tell Dad. Your ever-loving brother, Jim

Signed Jim Neat

CASE-NOTES (cont.)

Monday 16th December 1935

When asked about significant scar tissue in the Achilles tendon area, Jim explained that he underwent many operations for a club foot during the first five years of his life. Although this remained problematic throughout his youth, it appears to have healed well and affects him only slightly now.

He also suffered seriously from asthma, but reports that it improved as soon as he ran away to sea, aged fifteen.

He travelled extensively round the world before emigrating to Canada ten years ago. He had high expectations but, due to the economic conditions of our time, drifted into bad habits and has been forced to live a nomadic life.

Unemployed for the last six months, he has gone hungry on many occasions, resulting in a suspected duodenal ulcer, exacerbated by sporadic drug use.

During the fall, he was living rough in Toronto and arrested on many occasions, leading to frequent short prison sentences. I have acquired his jail records; he was convicted of vagrancy or drunkenness seven times within a space of four months. His last arrest was deliberately engineered, when he ordered and ate a full meal in a good down-town restaurant, then asked the waiter to call the police, as he was unable to pay. A day after he had served his sentence for this crime, he over-dosed on impure heroin. Found by police on a sidewalk in freezing temperatures in a very poor state, he was brought here.

He is still unable to speak of the circumstances that led him to such depths. I am familiar with the hobo's need to find a roof over his head during the winter and his willingness to break the law to achieve this end. I have a strong feeling in this case that something else triggered Jim's collapse, but I cannot put my finger on it.

He continues to attend Mrs MacTaggart's classes, slowly revealing the deteriorating circumstances that brought him here. She says he still destroys much of his writing, or crosses out the most painful recollections. (See attached)

D. Fletcher

Mam Died

January 1927

I've saved enough to send Mam a hundred dollars for Christmas: 'Don't worry about me,' I write to her, 'You should see my muscles! And I sleep like a log!'

A letter from dad two months later: 'Your mam lived to read your letter and was so proud of the dollars you sent, she declared she'd never spend them. ~~But, it pains me to tell you, dear boy, she died soon after.~~

~~'We helped her bear her kidney pain but at the end her there was nothing we could do to help her breathe. The saddest moment of my life when, gasping for air, she looked at me and said, "I will miss you so much Ruben, my love"".~~

~~I cry like a boy. Mam's death? Dad's sadness? My failures? Confusion leaves me empty, depleted of any knowledge of who I am, what I'm doing.'~~

Signed Jim Neat

19

East West

1928

Freight train heading west
is shunted into town.
I shove, am shoved.
Bulls* order the driver on.
I slink away
alongside the trucks
co-ordinate speed to perfection
grab an arm, am hauled
on board.

Talk is of Vancouver
warmer, logging, work-camps.
Squashed into a space
the size of Mam's scullery
we play harmonicas
sing Spivanky, O Canada
God save the King.
Almost happy.

Rockies erupt
blot out the sky
vanish.
Stench of faeces and vomit
hangs in the bitter air.
We pass a train two miles long
going east
men riding the rods
or clinging to the roof
~~men who didn't get work~~
~~where we're headed~~

Signed Jim Neat

*the railroad police, known for their brutality to hobos.

Undressing the Dead

Vancouver 1929

Men of the Jungle, we sit in silence on the shore of Burrard Isle. Too weary to protest we groan about the mess Prime Minister Bennett's made, how we'd manage the affairs of state a bloody sight better if we had his millions, his private education.

We sit poking small fires, sharing stews and narcotics to numb the pain. I must escape this brotherhood of ailing flesh. But I need a coat. I root through a bundle of clothes in a trailer. ~~It's solid . . . a man, already dead. I undress him.~~

Signed Jim Neat

West East

Vancouver to Saskatoon, March, 1930

In the middle of the night I slip out of that inhospitable city
(three months, without a roof over my head), head for the
railroad station. Rumours of farm work in Calgary. I ditch
Dickens, hang onto Conrad. Stuff pockets with tobacco, a
piece of soap, razor, pencil, knife, tin cup, a bag of sugar,
stolen.

Come out from my hiding place through a hole in the fence,
just as the train starts to roll out of the station heading east, I
run alongside, keep my feet as far from the rails as I can, catch
hold of the vertical steel door handle, heave myself sideways
onto the ladder, climb up on top. High risk, riding the rods in
winter. Try not to breathe going through the tunnels. Can't
get relief at Jaspar, stay hidden, platform heaving with Bulls.
Don't think about tomorrow.

After two days, body aching, longing for stillness more than
anything on earth, the mountains drop suddenly away, the
temperature rises, I'm enveloped in warm soft prairie
sunshine.

Jump down when the train stops, move around, relieve
myself, try and find water.

Edmonton, at last. But it's all lies, there is no work. We're
rounded up, herded off to another work-camp. Sometimes
there's opium, in exchange for food. My mind black as soot.

One day, I drift away, not caring what the mounted police
might do to me, keep walking, past farms and homesteads half
obliterated by drifted dust.

Reach North Battleford, drag myself onto a freight train headed for Saskatoon, nice warm boxcar, safe for a few hours, not suspecting for a second this mindless action will change my life forever.

Draw into Saskatoon railroad station, middle of the night, settle down to sleep in a corner of the platform. A porter, young black man (unusual sight in these parts) shows me into the smoking room, 'you'll be more comfortable in here,' he says, brings me hot coffee, we talk most of the night, have a lot in common, 'you'll get work in Saskatoon,' he says, 'we has local government projects for the unemployed, keeps you out of mischief, stops you coming a commie.' We laugh, tears pouring.

Signed Jim Neat

~~The Carpet~~

~~Saskatoon 1932~~

~~I climb the steps~~
~~to a grand front door; two bells,~~
~~one for the master, one for the maid.~~
~~'Any chores?' I ask the Fraulein with freckles~~
~~who peeps through the crack -~~
~~'in exchange for some food?'~~
~~'Take vot you vont,' she replies, leading me~~
~~by the hand~~
~~along the tiled hall, thrusting me~~
~~into the pantry.~~

~~On the soft sofa she smiles.~~
~~Blutwurst burns my throat.~~
~~A hot thigh fidgets next to mine.~~
~~The unaccustomed sweetness of her bee-sting cake~~
~~has me retching on my knees.~~
~~The smile fades.~~
~~'The carpet!' She shrieks~~
~~'I vill be sacked~~
~~Please leave at vonce!'~~

Signed Jim Neat

Miss Thomas

O Miss Thomas, of the School for Crippled Poor Boys. It was you ignited my imagination. With your stories of adventure, Treasure Island, Moonstone and Moby Dick, you flooded my little desk, I was drowning in them, till I met Lord Jim. And with him in my pocket I left home. See me race through the wet streets at dawn.

Four years a merchant sailor, at sea with Joseph Conrad, rusty water dripping on my bunk. When I abandoned ship in Cape Town, who did I blame, O Miss Thomas of such very fine intentions?

I cry out loud to Canada, O Canada, you promised me I'd reap rewards, find a wife, quickly rise to fame. You asked for migrant workers but your system's stacked against me. From coast to coast, I sawed spruce in freezing temperatures. Threshed grain in heat no one could stand. Got beaten up by bulls for riding steel rails I'd laid myself. Swept snow. Built roads. Bridges. Buried cattle. Did my goddam best.

Now we're offered jungles. Or gaol if we're lucky. Christ O Christ Canada your pernicious propaganda had best been left unsaid. Lord Jim. Fighting his past. Stripped of his papers.

Signed Jim Neat

The Book Store

Saskatoon 1932

MEN URGENTLY REQUIRED
TO COMPLETE BUILDING OF BESSBOROUGH HOTEL
SIGN ON AT TOWN HALL

'Married men only. Try reading the small print,' the town
clerk says, over the top of his glasses as if I stink, which I do,
'and you have to have proof.'

'Go to hell,' I say, and head for the university where I know
I'll get a meal for free.

I cross 25th Street Bridge. The river smelling sweet is wide
and running smooth. I turn into Clarence Avenue, see Heart
of Darkness in the window of a second-hand bookstore, step
inside. 'Hi there!' A woman's voice sings out from the back,
'be with you in a second!'

My wife?

Signed Jim Neat

CASE-NOTES (cont.)

Tuesday 20th December 1935

A postcard from Jim's sister in England (see attached), forwarded to him today from Toronto Gaol, refers to the death of a Lizbietta and to the whereabouts of a baby.

So now we know.

In our meeting this afternoon, I handed him the postcard. He stared at me a full minute, then started to shake and sob. I let him cry until he was spent then walked with him back to Cottage 11, where I knew Frank Schofield would be working at his typewriter.

Frank made us tea and we sat round the stove. I told Frank that Jim was recently bereaved and would probably appreciate some company tonight. They have more misfortune in common than I realized.

D. Fletcher

12th December 1935

Darling Boy

Still modelling, AS YOU CAN SEE! Don't I look stunning? But how shocked I was to read your news. Lizbietta dead? What happened? What happened to the baby?? I told Dad, couldn't keep such dreadful news to myself (don't worry, I didn't mention drugs or jail). I've met a lovely man who owns a huge house in Folkestone, close-by the seaside. Come home, stay with us, dear boy, imagine the fun we'll have!

Your ever-loving
Baby Queen

January 16th 1936

Just before Christmas, I took it upon myself to write to Jim's surprising sister (*see attached*). I received a prompt reply (*see attached*).

D. Fletcher

ONTARIO

THE ONTARIO HOSPITAL

Whitby, Ont., December 24th, 1935.

Miss Queenie Neat,
5 Wolfington Road,
West Norwood, S.E. 27,
London, England.

Re: James Neat

Dear Madam:

Your letter addressed to the Toronto Gail was forwarded to us. Mr. Neat came to this hospital as a voluntary patient on December 12th. I must say that our history is that these habits are of very long duration, and prior to his leaving England. Under the circumstances it is somewhat doubtful whether or not a cure can be effected. However, I hasten to assure you that we will do our utmost to make him comfortable, and bring about recovery if possible.

If you are in a position to pay his maintenance here, the charges are £1 16s per week approximately.

Yours sincerely,

D. R. Fletcher, M.D.
Superintendent.

DRF/P

Reply:

5 Wolfington Road, West Norwood,
London, SE 27, England
12th January 1936

Dear Dr Fletcher

I would like to thank you most profusely for your letter of 24th December, writing on Christmas Eve itself showed me what a kind man you must be and how lucky my darling brother Jim is to be in your care.

It would seem best for him to stay with you in the Whitby Hospital until he is strong again. Towards this end, we are happy to pay you the $1.10c per week you mentioned. However, I hope you can arrange for him to be brought back to England, at your earliest possible convenience. He should never of left in the first place.

Meantime, please find enclosed a postal order for 16 shillings which I hope is a correct estimate to cover for one month.

Yours very sincerely,
Miss Queenie Lee-Neat

20th January 1936

Due to the regularity of the hospital diet and outdoor activities that we engage him in, Jim's physical condition has improved considerably, although he still is unable to reveal the truth behind his circumstances.

If we can get him to stabilize emotionally, it may be possible to obtain for him a deportation. To this end, I wrote to his sister again this evening (see attached).

Meanwhile it is essential that he is encouraged to maintain active co-operation with us, as we attempt to unravel and deal with his recent past.

D. Fletcher

The Whitby Hospital
Ontario

January 20th 1936

Dear Miss Lee-Neat,

Your letter of January 12th received and in reply I can say that your brother has started to co-operate with the hospital routine and is now in better physical health. He is fully participating in the advanced occupational therapies and recreational activities available in this hospital and so we can, with optimism, look forward to an improvement in his condition.

I must though emphasise that I am keen for him to stay with us until he has emotionally stabilised.

Eventually I would like to see him deported to England, providing you can personally guarantee to meet him off the ship and take him under your wing for a few months until he finds fulfilling work.

A great deal depends on his will-power. We do our best to encourage discourse and point out the dangers that lie ahead if he were to return to his use of illegal drugs.

I acknowledge receipt of your cheque for 16 shillings; it is much appreciated in these times of financial restraint; such contributions help us to maintain the running of the hospital as we wish it to be run.

Yours truly,

Donald Fletcher

February 1st 1936

Mrs MacTaggart has been encouraging Jim to write about his childhood, his running away from home at the age of 15. The results, fascinating (see attached).

D. Fletcher

Queenie and I Strike a Deal

1904

First there's Fred The Recluse, then Victor who dies, followed by five prim girls, each one primmer than the one before. What a nunnery our house is, till Queenie arrives, pretty as a picture and belle of the ball. Then me, ~~all crippled and congested, operated on year after year with insufficient chloroform, our Mam so scared she nearly dies.~~

Queenie it is who cares for me most, vows to fight off the bullies amused by my surgical boot, who lie in wait to topple me – 'so long,' she says, 'as you promise to keep my secrets, every one.'

And I do.

Signed Jim Neat

Play to Win

1916

Fred refuses to come down from the attic.
'Stay up here, little brother with me,' he says,
'learn the savage art of bare-knuckle boxing,
like Bill Neat, The Bristol Butcher.'

He dusts me up,
'come on, Jim, defend yourself.
Your Country Needs You!
Stay on the balls of your feet,
spin, spin!'

Late into the night I practise my footwork,
vicious uppercuts, lethal jabs.

~~Our Mam in tears,~~
we switch sometimes, to chess.
'Come on Jim,' he says, 'it's all the same.
Play to win. Fight to the end.'

Signed Jim Neat

The Nape of My Brother-in-Law's Neck

1917

They find my brother-in-law half-buried in mud, raving mad.
'An imbecile, a despicable coward,' his discharge papers say.

Eyes bulging, arms, legs, head jerking, he can't get out the
front door, scuttles on all fours behind the settee, mouth
opening, shutting, opening.

My oldest sister, his wife of two years, pulls out a chair for
him, 'Sit down, dear,' she says. His face smashes down onto
the table. Looking at me, she strokes the nape of his neck,
'Best you go on home, Jim.'

Signed Jim Neat

Wayward Ones

1919

Queenie turns up on the arm of a heavyweight. We're all sat down to tea – 'Meet Terry', she says, 'like our most esteemed ancestor, The Bristol Butcher, he can fell an ox with his left hand, and guess what, we got married today!'

I'm fired up, this means I'll get to perfect my left hook.

Family dismayed.

In no time at all, Baby Lola arrives. I spoil her rotten with shop-lifted chocolate. Earn a clip round the ear from the local constabulary.

Family appalled.

Our very own Queenie is crowned Beauty Queen of all London! Always practising her glamorous glances, abandons Terry, kissing her Baby Lola goodbye, squeals, 'I'm off to Paris'.

Family full up to here.

I too pack my bag, set off for the docks. Cape Town, Fremantle, Los Angeles, Toronto, no longer dreams.

Mam gives up the ghost.

Signed Jim Neat

Cape Town to Western Australia

1920

I count five sunrises
Through a tear in the tarpaulin
Before crawling out, getting frogmarched to the bridge.

'Hard labour or he's overboard,' Skipper says.
That's ok with me – donkey work on deck –
And I sleep in the open, my sleep
As deep as the Indian Ocean.

Dad you'd be proud!
I have Bill Neat biceps now
And Mam, the salt air's cleared my lungs,
My asthma's gone, and my twisted foot?
It's straight! *Jesus wept*, I cry out loud
To the silvery clouds, *I'm cured*.

Commotion on the bow, the skyline shattered
By a landscape spiked with cranes. *Australia*.

White stowaways are welcome,
Cheap labour's in demand.
The handsomest man you ever set eyes on
Is officially an Uglyman*,
Building bungalows for widows of The War,
Pretty young widows – and I'm walking out with Dawn,
Prettiest widow in town.

Signed Jim Neat

---

* The Uglyman's Association established in Western Australian in 1917 to provide
charitable relief for widows and children of The Great War.

CASE-NOTES (cont.)

March 2nd 1936

Jim has struck up a productive rapport with Frank Schofield and settled down remarkably well in Cottage 11. Frank's professionally involved in the diseases of cattle and, on arrival here last year, he straightway started experimental work at our on-site farm, of which he, and indeed all of us, are now very proud. Earlier this week he explained his research project to Jim.

Dairy Herd and Barn at Whitby Hospital, 1930s

This has brought about an astonishing turning point in Jim's recovery. He is up at dawn, dealing with the dairy herd's every need. He is physically much improved, putting on weight and his stomach inflammation has subsided without recourse to surgery.

We have learned a little about his childhood in London and his extensive travels before emigrating to Canada. But he has still not spoken of his girlfriend, whose death, I believe, triggered his breakdown.

I have asked Frank to pry a little, when Jim is off guard in the evenings, but so far to no avail.

D.Fletcher

April 16th 1936

Our patient continues to attend Mrs MacTaggart's Writing Group on Thursday afternoons. We find the attached papers quite remarkable:

FAO Dr Fletcher

I asked Jim to write his memories of any homecoming he could remember. My only stipulation, as always, that he use the present tense. To me, it reads like a poem. In it, he refers to his girlfriend's diary. In spite of it being his only possession, he lent it to me, to read alongside 'The Homecoming'. He gave me permission to pass it on to you. I think you'll find both items of interest and suggest you read the diary first.

Signed:
J MacTaggart

LIZBIETTA'S DIARY

17th April 1932

A man with an English accent came in the store this afternoon, took Heart of Darkness out of the window, sat on the settee at the back and read all afternoon, having checked – 'Sure you don't mind? Because I can't pay, don't have a dime.' I made him a coffee, so I guess he felt welcome.

He wore a massive overcoat tied at the waist with binder twine and looked half-starved. Wish I'd asked him where he was from.

20th April 1932

He came in again today, that monstrous coat sodden with snow. Secret Agent this time.

21st April 1932

Told Valentyna about him. 'Holy smoke!' she shrieked, 'he'll be riding the rods, coming from nowhere, going no place. Leave well alone, honey.'

I asked her if Viktor had a spare sweater. She shut the stove down for the night and answered with her back to me: 'Spare sweater? Not sure that he does.' Later, when I came up to bed, I noticed she'd put one out for me on the attic stairs. Of course Viktor has a spare goddam sweater!

22nd April 1932

He told me he left England when he was 17, spent years at sea, before emigrating here in 1926, hoping to be allocated a prairie farm but, with the drought and depression, was reduced to endless rail-roading. Has farmed, laid rails and lumber-jacked, but there's nothing now. Said he'd see me tomorrow, unless he's offered a job interview. I hooted.

1st May 32

Valentyna said it was okay for him to move in. I could see he was getting ill – he'd been sleeping at the railroad station. It's been 35 below for a week. Now he's on the spare mattress in the hallway.

Valentyna and Viktor are worried about taking in a hobo. But, refugees themselves, they never turn away immigrants who've fallen on hard times. It's how the Ukrainian and Polish communities round here operate.

Started set of new drawings.

9th May 1932

Spring. Suddenly the air balmy. I've been coughing for months, just hope this wonderful warmth puts me right again.

Jim gets up early and walks to the grocery store to get Valentyna's supplies for the day. Serge and Zenaida love him being around; he plays the fool and teaches them card tricks. But one trick, where he sticks scraps of cigarette papers onto a knife, makes them appear and disappear, he won't explain to them, drives them nuts.

18th May 32

He's running the boarding house for Valentyna now! Frees her up to help Viktor with his fur trade, the only business left in town. She oversees the examination of this season's wild pelts, while he develops his mad plan for a silver fox farm.

Jim cooks for the students; made a stack of maple syrup flapjacks tonight. They're fascinated by his knowledge of the outside world, what a breath of fresh air in this dustbowl he is.

And he's fixed the privy roof that's been leaking for years.

Tonight he showed me his copy of Lord Jim. His favourite sister, Queenie, gave it to him before he came to Canada. Inside the front cover there's a photo of her when she was crowned May Queen of London in 1919. So pretty. He adores her.

20th May 32

He asked me last night how old I was when I came to Canada. I told him I was born in Vancouver – soon after my mother emigrated from Kiev in about 1909 but she died young and I have no memories of her, only Valentyna. I think they were friends. He asked so many questions and I had no answers, but afterwards, I started to remember the day Valentyna tried to explain to me that I wasn't her true daughter. I didn't want to know and rudely shut her up.

Now fragments keep coming back to me, how bad my mother felt about leaving her mother behind in a remote Ukrainian village, how they designed a system for staying in touch, as my Babushka could neither read nor write. I couldn't sleep for wondering about her. Funny, I really want to know now. Must ask Valentyna for more memories.

Sunday 25th May 1932

Supper finished, dishes washed and put away, we walked down to the river, watched the chipmunks for ages, taking dry grass down into their little burrows. Scrambled down the steep bank to the sandy beach below.

Afterwards we came back to my room. 'Best day of my life,' he said. Same was true for me. Jesus.

9th August 1932

The silver fox farm's collapsed – so Valentyna's home again. That makes Jim's position here untenable.

She told us this evening that both my mother and my grandmother were called Mariya, meaning Star of the Sea. Jim loved that, said one day we'd maybe have a daughter and live by the sea. He must miss the sea. Here the heat's so dense it's hard to breathe. Black dust storms day and night. Pack wet rags round all the windows but it's impossible to keep the dirt out. Last week an invasion of locusts devastated the crops and ate the underpants on our neighbour's washing line.

9th October 1932

He's gone north for logging work. First time we've been apart in six months.

He wanted me to go with him – said there's work for women in the canteens but I resisted the temptation to be with him at all costs. Although my job teaching at the university fell through because the government cut all courses except agriculture, I can still earn a lot more in the bookstore, and live free with Valentyna. And, although I don't have materials to develop my sculpture project, at least I get the chance to draw and plan works for the future. Am running out of drawing books.

He's more insecure than I am, finds it hard to believe I love him. I can't believe how much I do, how much я скучаю за ним, and his lop-sided smile.

16th February 1933

At last, a letter. Conditions there dire. Temperature 40 below all January; his state of mind rock bottom.

Logging will finish at the end of April when transport out of the forest will be organised. If he can hang on that long, he'll return to Saskatoon and I won't let him suffer like this again.

He said at least he'll have a decent pay packet to bring back. If we add that to my savings from the bookstore, we'll be able to stay on here till the spring, get well again, his stomach, my cough.

July 1933, Eldon

Holy cow! We're farming! In Eldon, 150 miles west of Saskatoon. After Viktor's fur business collapsed, Valentyna heard that all university courses were being been cut, so no new students in September, no lodgers. Both their incomes gone.

Then a miracle. Adam, the black porter at Saskatoon railroad station who'd befriended Jim, asked us to help his mother run this homestead – arranged for us to travel by horse and trap owned by the black pioneer community, took us two days, we lay out in the open at night, felt like we were on the roof of the world and the stars looking down on us all night so bright we couldn't sleep.

We live in the sod-house that Adam's parents built as their first shelter when they arrived from Oklahoma in 1909. Adam's mother, Grace, and his grandparents live in the main lumber house just fifty yards away.

There are woods nearby, so we're never short of logs for cooking and heating. We have a milk cow (bony, beautiful Sappho), two hogs, chickens, geese, a beehive, an apple orchard, a garden and ten acres of farmland. Share the horse and other equipment with two families who live nearby.

August 1933

Adam's grandmother taught me how to harvest the honey. Gave 30lbs to our neighbours in return for wheat.

September 1933

We keep charts, maps and diaries, record what we sow, plant and reap. Document milk yield and egg production and Jim thinks we're improving on it. We have no need of money. Once in a while Adam brings tea, coffee, sugar, tobacco and the grandparents' medicine from Saskatoon.

Jim's proud of the muscles I'm developing.

29th October 1933

The geese died. We were caught out by an early frost, found them frozen solid, huddled together against the fence. We shared them around the community, for broiling. Mortified.

5th December 1933

Jim's twenty ninth birthday. Snowed in by perfect snow. Played chess all afternoon.

We think we've enough produce and cider for two months. We've brought Sappho indoors which keeps her alive and the soddy warm but there are drawbacks – shit.

We cook supper in Grace's kitchen and all five of us eat together in the evenings – vegetable stew, potatoes, pumpkin pie. On rare occasions a prairie chicken or bush rabbit, but this only if we've negotiated an exchange with a neighbour, as neither of us is very good at killing.

He distempered over the pages of old magazines for me to use as sketchbooks – a great surface to work on. Have finished a stack nearly a foot high already. He reads. Conrad. Shaw. Lawrence. Dickens. Wells.

Grandpa and grandma both weak. The doctor visited in the fall, but we shan't see him again till spring.

12th January 1934

Worried sick by Jim's wheezing and coughing. Inhalations of wild mint before bed is helping. Read to him from Little Dorrit. My English accent made him laugh so much I thought he was going to bust a lung. No tobacco since December.

10th February 1934

Jim took the horse and sledge to Digby Woods to fell birch for fuel. He tied a pillow with binder-twine to his chest, underneath his coat, to keep warm while driving. I laughed so hard to see my slim Jim fat, I wet myself, no laughing matter in these temperatures. He said the trees shattered like glass when he axed them.

16th February 1934

Temperature dropped 15 degrees within a few minutes yesterday. We woke to find snow had drifted between our shack and Grace's. A long beautiful wave that reached up to the eaves. Saw smoke coming from her chimney, so knew they were okay. Stayed in bed most of the day. This evening we cut our way through, took them soup.

21st February 1934

Grandpa died on Saturday. Adam came for the funeral at the Shiloh Church, which Grandpa helped build in 1910. All the neighbours came. Adam placed white stones at each end of the grave. Grandma wept all the way to the church but afterwards, on the way home, said she was glad to be leaving him in such a beautiful place. We spent the rest of the afternoon looking at photos and talking about their early days on the homestead. She gave me a photo of Grandpa standing by Caesar, their son, (Adam's Pa) – he died of flu in 1918, when he was thirty three, so sad – they're standing on their homestead, where we're now growing carrots and turnips. And a beautiful studio photograph of Grace, taken just before they left Oklahoma.

17th March 1934

Store cupboard almost empty. Adam sent us cash last week, so Jim's taken the horse and buggy to Lloydminster to stock up. Trips out like this take days.

19th March 1934

He's back, with coffee and tea, Ely's Cream Balm for our coughs; Sulphose Vaginal Suppositories for grandma. And tobacco. Bees have survived the winter.

21st June 1934

Valentyna and Viktor arrived in a Bennett Buggy*. They stayed two nights, drank a lot of cider.

Their involvement with the Ukrainian Labour Temple Association disqualifies them from any relief and the Communist Party's been outlawed.

Gave them eggs and cider to take back.

29th June

Heat wave; I wear just my cotton frock and go bare-foot most the time; Jim's rigged up a shower; a leaky bucket on a branch.

29th October 1934

No period last week and been throwing up every morning. So happy I've just jumped up onto the window sill.

15th November 1934

All night long Jim wraps himself around our baby and me. He says he'll read to me from Conrad when I go into labour. I dream about the river.

2nd December 1934

Adam's lost his job. He'll have to come back to the homestead. Jim and I'll have to return to Saskatoon. I know Valentyna won't

---

* A car that had its engine knocked out and was pulled by a horse.

refuse us shelter but, with none of us earning a dime, we're scared for the baby. Last night Jim dreamed he was following an arrow in a forest, desperately searching for something, when he realized the arrow was sticking out of his chest. It had been fired into him from behind.

5th December 1934

Jim's thirty today and Adam has returned, with his bride, Philomena, a beautiful Metis girl. She's mixing a herbal paste from the prairie to rub into my pregnant belly skin.

16th April 1935, Saskatoon

Returned in January, so here I am in Queen Street, where I grew up. Valentyna, who to all intents and purposes, adopted me when I was one month old, is happy to have me back. But Jesus, how I miss Jim and our year and a half in the promised land.

He left to join a tree planting project in Regina six weeks ago, not heard from him since. Most letters get lost or are long-delayed in their delivery these days, I know that. But I'm tormented, care only for him and our unborn child.

I'm sure it's a girl, and we'll call her Mariya, Star of the Sea, and she's going to be a writer. Jim says it's a boy (Adam) and he's going to be boxer. We have to disagree on something.

Dark clouds of dust are hanging in the streets. Been coughing for weeks. It helps to hold a wet cloth over my face.

25th May 1935

A letter. Says he's saved nearly 80 dollars, will definitely be back in time for the baby.

Valentyna and Viktor are leaving soon for Ontario. They say there's plenty of work for Ukrainians in the nickel mines in that area, that we should all go and live there. I'll look after Zenaida and Serge while they're away. That's no problem, I adore their company.

1st June 1935

It's impossible to stay cool. I dream of rain. I'm so huge and exhausted, can't find the energy to work in my sketchbooks anymore. I miss the kids during the day while they're at school and miss Jim holding me and our baby all night long.

Saturday 15th June 1935

Jim should be back by now; must be caught up in riots. Read in the Star Phoenix that a railroad trek of unemployed men from Vancouver, protesting at the conditions in the work-camps, was halted in Regina. They'd been trying to get to Ottawa to confront the Bennett administration. RCMP charged with no provocation – men were killed, hundreds thrown in jail.

I've been searching in vain for the familiar outline of his body in the newspaper photographs. None of them goddam clear enough.

Wednesday 24th June 1935

Viktor and Valentyna due back today but I got word they been held up by strikes in Winnipeg.

The diary ends here.

The Homecoming 1935

I get back to Saskatoon with $80 in my pocket for Lizbietta but she is dead, it's 40 degrees, the curtains are drawn, she died five days ago, Valentyna tells me, we buried her by the river, tuberculosis, post-partum haemorrhage, I don't know, I don't know, but bleeding, unstoppable bleeding, Valentyna's sobbing, I shake her, she falls to the floor, I pull her to her feet, the baby, she says, they took the baby to an orphanage, they say you can't see her because you're of no fixed abode, I'm running, Valentyna follows me, down Queen Street, to the Bethany Home for Unmarried Girls and Illegitimate Babies, I hammer on the fortified door, women in uniform push me down the steps, doors slam, bolts yanked across, I break a window, blood and glass, I'm handcuffed, in the North Battleford Hospital for the Insane, in a strait-jacket, my mouth so dry I can't speak, Viktor arrives, I weep, come on Jim, he says, don't die in a lunatic asylum for Christ's sake, for her sake, would she want you to die in this hell-hole? come on, Valentyna told me to tell you when the baby's older, we can adopt her, come back with me, Jim, we'll go east, we'll get mining work, if you can only pull yourself together, the barbiturates wiping me out, he asks a nurse, can't he be discharged, no, he's a danger to himself and others, to be detained indefinitely, Viktor sits on my bed, holy smoke, Jim, he says, I won't be able to come again, you'll have to get yourself out this shit-hole, he puts a packet on my chest, you'll want this, he says, look after it son, just get out of here quick as you can, he's gone, I sleep, wake up, the packet, still lying on my chest, Jesus wept, it's Lizbietta's diary, I focus, I read, I'm sane, I creep round the ward past patients sleeping two to a bed, too comatose to care, I steal a pair of trousers from one, a jacket from another, but there are no shoes, I escape through a back window before dawn, the night's warm, I'm free, walk barefoot to the train-station, hide in a tunnel till dark, hoist myself up onto a long-distance boxcar slowly passing through, swallow a handful of pills, wake up, a day, two days later, sprawled in a siding, beaten up by bulls, boxing skills dead, can't stand, can't open my eyes, holes in my mouth where my teeth should be, can't remember, Toronto Jail vagrancy, Toronto Jail drunk, August, September, October, November, I don't know, one night, so cold, in a restaurant, pork tenderloins, a bottle of wine, I tell the waiter, call the police, I can't pay, instead, he calls an ambulance, I wake up, find myself here

Signed Jim Neat 11th April 1936

CASE-NOTES (cont.)

Thursday 23rd April 1936

Jim is proving a most valuable example of the viability of our current therapeutic practices. My research in Germany and the USA four years ago is paying dividends.

We are seeing very favourable results, with no medical or surgical intervention whatsoever, in cases of trauma and depression; no dungeons, no barred windows.

The dark days of prison-like facilities at institutions such as The Toronto Asylum for the Insane are surely over. I try to influence the new Medical Superintendent there by submitting case-notes to him of patients who have benefited from our experimental approach, in the hope that he will adopt similar practices.

All our wards are built as separate Cottages, each one set in a bucolic landscape, housing a small number of patients and in receipt of direct sunlight.

The village-like setting, with winding avenues and trees, over-looking and sloping down gently to the shores of Lake Ontario, is not just a romantic ideal. Every day I see patients' interest in life returning; simply being given the independence to make themselves a cup of coffee in the cottage kitchen when they feel like it, gives them a degree of self-respect that has hitherto been denied them.

We are particularly proud of the farm, now fully operated by the patients and staff; 400 acres of fertile land providing supplies to the hospital, significantly helping to keep costs down. Sufficient grain crops are grown to feed livestock. The cattle provide enough milk for staff and patient needs. Meat requirements are met by the chickens and pigs.

The Barn at Whitby, 1930s, largest in Ontario

There are 75 acres of vegetable garden and fruit orchard, the produce being canned or pickled in our on-site cannery. Patients are paid wages and given tobacco rations. Everybody wins. In a time of severe depression, our patients eat like gods.

Jim makes excellent use of these opportunities and I am convinced now of a successful outcome.

D. Fletcher

Wednesday 29th April 1936

We are all delighted with Jim's progress. He has availed himself of our dentistry department, had his teeth fixed and is a handsome man, unrecognisable from the lop-sided wreck that turned up five months ago.

It is proving a stroke of genius that we put him in the same cottage as Frank Schofield. Although Frank's faith undisputedly bestows a calming influence, it is his Holstein research programme that is having the greatest impact on Jim's rehabilitation – the aim of which is to establish the cause of the hemorrhagic disease in cattle that has been spreading across Ontario in recent years. Frank believes that it is not an infectious disease, but caused by a mold in sweet clover silage.

He carries out tests on the cattle and Jim catalogues the results for Frank to analyse. Keeping his mind focused on endless lists of data related to milk yield, weather conditions and types of clover eaten, is helping him to stabilize. He responds well to structure and purpose. A very nice symbiosis indeed.

D. Fletcher

Thursday 30th April 1936

His most recent writing demonstrates a more cohesive thought process and marked improvement in his ability to connect empathically: what extraordinary progress in his growing self-awareness and sensitivity to others.

When he learned, however, of the murder of one of our male nurses here last year (see attached) he became heavy of heart for several days.

In the second attachment he relates a conversation with our own dear Frank Schofield, from which I've learned details of Frank's history that I should myself have gleaned from him many months ago.

D. Fletcher

Murdered Lad of Penge

There's a photograph in the hospital library, on the wall above
this desk – a young man, in his Sunday best, standing by the steps
of the Nursing School.

Who's that? I ask. Ethelbert Rich, the librarian says,
poor lad, was an orderly here.
Why poor? He looks all right to me.
Strangled with his own neck tie, she says, by a patient,
delusional, convinced Ethelbert had poisoned his coffee.

I read the inscription:
born in Penge – Jesus, that's where I was born.
in 1904 – Jesus Christ – that's when I was born.

I peer into the face. Christ Almighty,
I reckon we've passed each other a hundred times
en route to the Featherweight Boxing Club
off Crystal Palace Parade.

I'm sorry you came out here to die, Ethelbert.
I have to live, to keep Lizbietta alive but you,
who, in Penge, keeps you alive?

Signed Jim Neat

Ethelbert Rich, murdered in Cottage No 14, 1933

Frank Schofield's God

We sit in the kitchen talking late into the night. How the hell have I ended up in the company of this man? We both came to Canada years ago, to seek our fortunes. He's Professor of Bacteriology at Ontario Veterinary College, I'm a hobo, destitute drug addict, ex-convict. And here we are, huddled around a wood-stove in Cottage 11, both bereaved, in a hospital for the insane.

I'm going to write down our conversation, as accurately as I can because I don't ever want to forget it. I don't expect I can do justice to his wisdom but I'll try.

He caught poliomyelitis when he was nineteen — that left him partially paralysed so he was unable to fight in the Great War. He was sent to Korea instead, to teach Bacteriology at the Medical College in Seoul.

> I had to go, Jim, I had no choice, but Alice, my wife, it was an error of judgement on my part to insist that she came with me, one that destroyed her life, one I deeply regret.
>
> We'd only been married a year. She was eighteen, a promising pianist; such sweet music she played! I'd become so used to the delights of her small body I wanted her to travel with me, to be beside me. But we had no idea what we were letting ourselves in for. You see, Jim, I betrayed her — by falling in love with the Korean people and becoming involved in their struggle.

I didn't know anything about Korea, so Frank explained that it had been under Japanese rule for years and when he saw how terribly the Koreans were suffering, he decided to join the fight for their liberation.

> I left her for days, then weeks, on her own, without even her piano for company, while I committed myself more and more to the cause. I

visited prisons and treated the tortured. I ignored her pleas that I stay at home. I assumed she would learn to tolerate my obsession. But she became hysterical, took to her bed, stopped eating.

I was called away to the scene of a village massacre, a reprisal for the killing of one Japanese policeman. I took photographs, treated the female survivors. There were only five.

When I got back to Seoul I discovered that the ministry had taken it upon itself to send Alice back to Toronto. I was angry, but what could I do? God had called me to help the Koreans. You have to understand that, Jim, it was a calling.

It scares me that Frank lets God make decisions for him.

I arranged a meeting with the Prime Minister of Japan, complained to him about the dictatorship's treatment of innocent Korean citizens. I showed him photographs of the torture victims I'd treated. But the regime used the photographs as evidence of treachery and they imprisoned me, deported me a year later. I had failed.

Back in Canada I learned that Alice had been with child when she'd been sent home. Her parents mistook her despair for madness and she was committed to the Toronto Asylum for the Insane. I was told she died in childbirth there – but that I had a son of six months, in an orphanage. I released him, raised him myself. But I was a broken man, Jim, not at all a good father.

The night's so quiet we can hear waves on the shore of the lake. And my heart, I can hear my heart. So what are you doing here, Frank, a patient?

I was angry that I hadn't convinced anyone that governments were involved in a cover-up in Korea. I was tormented by the loss of my wife. I wasn't fit to raise a child. I lost faith in God. I was finished.

I reheat the coffee on the stove. Trying not to think about his wife, I ask him if he misses his son.

I focus on my research. I go into a private world where I remember the good times. I recreate them in precise detail. It works for me because my trust in a Loving Father has returned to me and I know now I'll pull through and get back to my son.

I have no interest in Frank's God or any other. But he's made me realize I can recreate a world where I'm still with Lizbietta. I'm determined not to survive by forgetting her. That's the last thing I want to do, lose the memory of her laughter, how she laughed when she came, every time. Only I know those things; if I stop remembering them, she really will die. I am her rememberer. That's my job now. Jesus Wept.

I see her walking towards me, her cotton dress soaking wet; she's just thrown a bucket of water from the well over herself. She's smiling. Earlier she'd said she was sure she was pregnant. Her wet arms go round my neck. She's telling me she's never been so happy.

This evening, I press my face against the warm flank of a healthy Holstein, milk gushing into the pail, remember Sappho, our one poor cow, how bony her back was that last fall, how thin her yield, her pleading eyes. I don't cry. I start to train my thoughts.

Signed Jim Neat

CASE-NOTES (cont.)

Saturday 23rd May 1936

We were alarmed by Jim's disappearance for two days, immediately after he had written about Frank. When he returned he informed us that he had visited the Toronto Asylum, on a hunch that Frank's wife was still alive and reported that she is indeed confined there to this day.

Frank was initially confused and grief-stricken but today has shown signs of interest at the prospect of being reunited with his wife.

D. Fletcher

Toronto Asylum for the Insane (Metro Toronto Library)

Tuesday 26th May 1936

The release of patients into unsuitable environments is a major problem in this province and the next important issue I am going to tackle.

The political situation is of great concern to us all. The rise of fascism in Europe is evident on our own streets; the government's paranoia around communism and the unions is encouraging those in power to close ranks with the rich, at the intolerable expense of the poor, the sick and the unemployed.

Our towns are crawling with troops instructed to clamp down on every 'undesirable'. Vulnerable people are to be rounded up – and will, I fear, disappear forever.

We cannot keep Jim here indefinitely but I will never allow such patients to be discharged into an environment in which they are bound to regress and then be disposed of.

However, Frank (while dealing with his own precarious affairs), has friends in high places who, we hope, are securing a deportation order for Jim.

D. Fletcher

May 1936

Frank Schofield has been discharged. He is hoping to obtain the release and rehabilitation of his wife.

He and I remain in contact and are working towards securing a safe future for Jim (see attached).

Additionally, Frank tells me his veterinarian research is now focussed upon developing a drug for treatment of conditions where the clotting time of blood has to be increased, and is optimistic that it could be applied to humans as well as cows*. His time here has advanced his research in ways that could not have been anticipated and contributed to his recovery. How immensely gratifying.

D. Fletcher

---

* Schofield elucidated the etiology and pathology of mouldy sweet clover poisoning, which led to the discovery of the anticoagulant warfarin.

Ontario Veterinary College
(University of Toronto), Guelph, Ontario

Dear Miss Lee-Neat

Your brother and I met in this hospital last year, when I was recovering from a serious nervous breakdown. I could see he was a gentleman down on his luck. We struck up a friendship and have worked together towards our mutual recoveries.

I have returned to the above address, where I am Professor of Bacteriology. But I remain in close contact with your brother and am of the opinion that he needs to return to his home country, so long as you are in a position to support him.

I think he will pull through, but only if he can acquire a living faith in God as a loving Father who cares greatly for him. I have often tried to tell Jim of all that God did for me, but to no avail. So we must pray earnestly for him. Do not send him any money. Unfortunately Man is almost powerless of himself to break off the drug habit.

Having said that, I have learned a great deal from Jim and am deeply impressed with the strengths he has found within himself to counter the blows that life has dealt him. He is an invaluable friend to me, in ways I can't begin to describe.

I anticipate that he will be discharged from hospital within the next month. He will stay with me in Toronto until we have cleared his application for deportation.

I look forward to hearing from you,

Most sincerely,
Frank W. Schofield

C. D. McGILVRAY, V.S., M.D.V., D.V.SC.
PRINCIPAL

UNDER THE DEPARTMENT OF AGRICULTURE OF ONTARIO
AND
AFFILIATED WITH THE UNIVERSITY OF TORONTO

ONTARIO

ONTARIO VETERINARY COLLEGE
GUELPH, CANADA

Ap. 28. 36.

Dear Mrs Keat,

Your brother Jim has asked me to write
to you giving you some information as
to his condition. I can give you first hand
news as I saw him at Easter.
It is a long story as to how I got to
know him, but we met last year. I was
in a hospital recovering from a serious
nervous breakdown and Jim came
in voluntarily to break away from
the drug habit. I could easily see
that he was a gentleman, & that he
was badly up against it. From then
till now I have kept in touch with
him & will do so.
He left the hospital last Fall & got
work on a farm, but when the work
was over he came back to the city
& again began to take drugs. We got
him back in a hospital at Whitby
where there are many such cases. Then
again he left & because having no work

Reply:

Dear PROFESSOR Schofield!!

My father and I are delighted to hear that you have, through your eminant position and great diligence and generosity, seen fit in spite of your own serious break down and indisposition, to obtain a Deportation Order and to pay all expenses involved so enabling my brother to return to his native country and family, where he should by rights have stayed all along.

As requested, I am writing to insure you that we will be at Southampton Docks on July 24th, ready to welcome him home.

I am your truely grateful

Queenie Lee-Neat
c/o The Vaudeville Theatre, Strand, London

Tuesday 2nd June 1936

Jim is anxious to trace his young daughter and reunite her with the step-parents of his deceased girlfriend before he leaves the country. Sadly we have failed to trace either the child or grandparents.

In spite of this, his overall recovery is nothing short of miraculous. We are preparing to discharge him within the month.

D. Fletcher

Tuesday 30th June 1936

Jim was in positive frame of mind this morning. As well as carrying out his farm duties, he is setting up a new kitchen-garden project before he leaves. The aim is to supply the whole hospital, patients and staff, with all its fruit and vegetable requirements, throughout the year.

Additionally he and other patients are sowing a flower field – I do not know what their plans are for that exactly, but if it cheers us all up in these devilish times, it won't be a bad thing. They are even talking of bee-hives.

D. Fletcher

Saturday 4th July 1936

Jim was discharged at 10 am; he is heading for Toronto, where he will be met by Frank Schofield. I feel confident that our methods here at the Whitby have done Jim proud and that he, in turn, will not let us down. I have written to Queenie, his rather extraordinary sister (see attached).

Our modern therapeutic approaches are being vindicated day on day. It only remains for us to obtain the government funding necessary to make sure these facilities and treatments are available in all Canadian hospitals.

D. Fletcher

Donald Fletcher, 1937

The Whitby Hospital, Ontario
4th July 1936
Re: Mr Jim Neat

Dear Miss Lee-Neat

I am very pleased that I can write to you with the news that we discharged your brother today, in positive mood. We are immensely pleased with the progress he has made over the last nine months. A determination to overcome his addiction and an inherent strength of character enabled him to come to terms with the most appalling circumstances. We are proud of him.

As you know, Jim played an important role in new therapeutic practices that we employ in this hospital. He is a fine example of a traumatised patient to have benefitted from our approach. To continue with this work we need considerable funding and have yet to convince the Ontario authorities of our programme's efficacy. To this end, we have to submit an application containing evidence of successful patient outcomes. Your brother's case-notes and the poems he wrote while a patient here form the bulk of this evidence and I would like your permission to use them. I have provided him with duplicates as I believe they will be of value to him.

On a personal note, I would like to mention that your brother's presence in the hospital has even benefitted my wife, Daphne. I confide in you that having given birth to a stillborn child last year, she was deeply depressed and unable to participate in normal activities. It worried me that I was having success with my patients, but could do nothing for my wife. I had to leave her at home alone and set off on my bike, enthusiastic about the new therapies that were working so well just two miles down the road, in the knowledge that she could not so much as take one step outside the front door. She was scarcely eating. One day, I told her about Jim, showed her his poetry, explained that his case-notes, in my dreadful handwriting, would need to be typed up, for the funding submission. I saw a spark in her eyes, and she said she would like to be the one to do it. She became interested in Jim and his recovery and, having polished up her typing skills, has completed a thundering proposal, which includes Jim's poetry. I am optimistic we will be successful. And I'd like you to know that Daphne herself is writing daily and making grand progress.

I look forward to hearing from you,

Donald Fletcher

WAR

CORRESPONDENCES

Letters from Jim to Queenie 1937-1940

September 1936, West Norwood

Dearest Queenie, I cannot yet believe it – deported and penniless – I'm home. But without Mam, it doesn't feel like home. Her powder compact is still on her dressing table beside the bed where Dad still sleeps. How can he keep it there? How can he not, I suppose. It smells the same as it always did. I'm a stranger here Baby Queen. Can't wait to ride the rods to Folkestone. Expect me on Sunday.

Your ever loving brother
Jim

1st December 1936

Dearest Queenie, Crystal Palace is no more, you probably saw the flames from Folkestone. We were called out but our hoses failed. Nothing could be done. Thank you for the photo – what the hell was the production? What on earth are you up to?

Jim

26th March 1940

I'm sorry, Baby Queen. Distressing times. More cruel news I'm afraid. It's as well you didn't risk the journey to London for the funeral; it was cancelled due to air-raids and in the chaos afterwards the coffin was mislaid. The girls were beside themselves. But when the rubble's all been cleared away I'm sure we'll find it and bury our dad in decent manner.

Your loving brother
Jim

April 1940

Lost my job with the Fire Brigade. In an argument I spoke up for the Ukrainian national character, got sacked without pay. Don't know if they took me for a Communist sympathiser or a Nazi, or what. I'm neither and the world's gone mad. God Almighty, Queenie, I can feel almost glad Lizbietta's not here to see it.

Jim

June 1940, Pioneer Corps, Savernake Forest, Malborough

Queenie, I've met someone, a teacher, wild black hair, bewildering brown eyes, she was helping out in the canteen, sold me a packet of Craven 'A'. She said, until she met me, the nicest thing anyone had ever said to her was that she looked like Beethoven! She's called Kate, we hope to marry as soon as possible, can't wait to introduce you. Your ever-loving brother

Jim

Letters from Kate to her Friend Molly, 1940-41

September, 1940

He's a widower. Or so he told me, this evening. He married a girl in Canada, who died in childbirth – the baby daughter was taken away to an orphanage and he was never allowed to see her, because he was 'of no fixed abode' and 'deemed unsuitable'. Can you believe it? He wept and I really didn't know what to do. I do feel sorry for him.

I met his sisters last week, all six of them. Ye Gods! The youngest, Queenie, a flighty cabaret dancer with whom I have absolutely nothing in common, said, 'I hope you know what you're taking on!' The others (Violet, Victoria, Beatty, Hetty and Daisy), all prim girls working in service: 'Don't come to us with your problems, we've troubles enough of our own!' they warned me. But since I don't see eye to eye with any of them, on anything, I can't imagine that's going to be very likely.

November, 1940

Good Heavens, Molly, spare me his sisters! Queenie, his favourite, has just left. I'm exhausted. She seemed to feel the need to put me in the picture regarding her brother: 'How many surgical operations on his club foot by the time he was seven? Sixteen! Every time a cloth drenched in chloroform slapped over his face, the only thing between him and unbearable pain. No wonder he has a sweet tooth. Did you know chloroform's six times sweeter than sugar?'

Then I heard how on Sundays, the six sisters would dress him up in a long white frock to hide his surgical-boot and leg-iron: 'We'd stand him on the kitchen table, like a bleeding birthday cake! We'd beg him to sing – Give us a treat, Jim, sing for us, sweet as Victor used to sing?'

Victor was their cherished choir-boy brother, he died of appendicitis aged nine, just days before Jim was delivered. How in heaven's name was Jim going to follow that?

Queenie gave me this picture of the poor lad that died – that's her between his knees and one of the older sisters. An only child, I find I don't know how to handle all of this. Oh Molly, what have I done?

Christmas 1940, Clapham

I was at home with mother for Christmas – we were waiting for Jim to arrive – he had 24 hour leave – the atmosphere crackling with nerves – she wasn't at all comfortable with the idea of a man in my life (this was the first time they'd met) – not only that, but bombs were falling – the sky to the north was red as the city of London burned – we could hear fire engines and ambulances and aeroplanes all at the same time. When he entered the cold tiled hallway, out of breath, covered in dust, and the first thing he did was ask mother for my hand in marriage, she replied, after a rather long pause, 'Do as you will.'

So we did.

April 1941

I was already pregnant when we had our small wedding in Marlborough and brief honeymoon in Ross-on-Wye. Such things happen in wartime. It was all rather frantic and wonderful.

Activities that I found strange enough in the dark now occur in broad daylight, in the kitchen, on the floor; Molly, how is it, as soon as it's over, I want him to start again and he does?

Until, that is, the day he asked me, 'You sure you've never done this before?' and I said, out of frustration as much as anything, 'Yes, when I was a child of four, six, eight, ten, by my mother's boy friend.' And Jim, whose body had been lovingly entwined with mine, became a raging beast, stormed off half-clothed to London, where he confronted my mother who, not used to vile outbursts, closed the door gently but very coldly in his face and hasn't spoken to us since.

Selection of Jim's Postcards to Kate Interspersed with Pioneer Archives

WILTSHIRE

Underground Ammunition Depot*
Monkton Farleigh, June 1941

My beloved Kate

With the unaccustomed weight of an Enfield revolver hanging from my waist, I unload shells from trains onto conveyor belts and guide them through England's dark white tunnels. On night-duty, I sit alone in this vast bomb-proof crypt, cut off from the world above, its war, and you. Sweet Jesus, I miss you.

Here in my dim underworld, I fight the perfectly logical ban on cigarettes but give in and light up; half in tears I fall asleep, fag in hand smouldering, until my relief appears, a good friend as it happens, who, smelling smoke, for a joke, shouts – 'Fire!' I wake with a start and I fire and fire till red stars bright the dark, and fire consumes fire.

Yours forever, Jim

Savernake Forest, 216 Company

Darling Kate

The Coy was delivered a whole pig for Christmas dinner. Private Hog. Dressed up in full marching order and exhibited outside the Mess tent with a notice stuck in his belly, 'Joined 216 Coy PC on 24 Dec 1941. Soon got awfully cut up and left next day.' I'd rather have been at home with you. How are you? I cannot wait to hear your news. Still making roads through the forest but hope to get 24 hours leave next week,

Yours ever, Jim

* Written on the inside of a cigarette packet, found after Kate's death in 2009

ALGERIA

PIONEER ARCHIVES

At Algiers, our most westerly point, from a working population of 350,000 we have been successful in producing as much labour as required. Ammunition, Petrol and Engineer Stores are kept at MAISON CARREE, a market town eight miles away, which seems to possess an inexhaustible supply of verminous humanity. Feeling against the British runs high, and a great deal of beating around the countryside is required before labour flows in the required quantity.

c/o APO 4605, 26th April 1943

My beloved Kate, This might be my last chance to write for a while. Tonight we leave for a remote, un-named region. I have to sign every package I send, confirming that the contents don't breach wartime national security. If you don't hear from me for a month or two, please don't worry. Au revoir, as they say here. Missing you both so much, always yours, Jim

2nd May 1943

Beloved Kate, As Algeria is still part of France, we have to work with the existing government officials; they make this difficult for us, as they see the disappearance of the Germans as most unfortunate and they hope it's only temporary! My job is to account for wages paid to unskilled Arab labour, on massive sheets of paper filled with rows of thumb prints ... open to abuse by all.
Ever yours, Jim

28. - MAISON-CARRÉE. - L'Agence Commerciale et Rue du Marché

28th May 1943 On active service

My beloved Kate, I know this corner of Maison-Carree quite well, though it no longer has this peaceful appearance. It's the assembly point where the natives have to register for work early every morning. It takes them 2 or 3 hours to walk here from their village. My only good moments are when I dream of you. My love, Jim

8th August 1943

Beloved Kate, My current job as Works Supervisor is to recruit gangs of 25 (one foreman, 24 labourers), for reconstruction work. As we are so short of labour, we promised the job of foreman to anyone who could produce his own gang. Can you imagine the confusion? Soon we were inundated with so many unsatisfactory gangs and foremen that we had to renege on our promise very quickly. I'm missing kissing you so much and it's weeks since we received any post.
Yours ever, Jim

28/8/43

My beloved Kate, We spend days scrambling up the winding goat tracks of the high Algerian hills to remote villages. We entice small parties of 10 or 12 down with promises of excellent pay – but when they hear the scream of falling bombs, they take flight back to the security of the hills and we have to start our task all over again. Their main concern is to protect their vineyards; far more important to them than the outcome of the North African campaign – can't blame them.
Ever yours, Jim

13/9/43

Dearest Kate, Today I found a boy, hiding alone in the mountains. He was so scared, had no understanding of the war or who we were. With the few words of Arabic that I've learnt and some French, I persuaded him to join us and we drove him back to his village. But I think of the bombs falling in London, and you cowering under the kitchen table. I should be there, not here, I should be with you. All my love and kisses, Jim

16/9/43

Dearest Kate, At last we've got through to the area where we're needed. We're rebuilding roads, reconnecting the water supply and distributing sacks of grain. It feels good to be working hard and to see the value of it for once. I love you every minute of every day, Yours forever Jim

SICILY

PIONEER ARCHIVES

On the eve of sending our men on to Sicily, it is important to recognise that they were Pioneers in the true sense when they arrived in Algeria – since they worked without precedence or guidance and broke a trail on which the highways of Civil Labour will eventually be built.

We have learned lessons from the mistakes made in North Africa that will help us enormously in the challenge that lies ahead.

8th October 1943

News at last; safely delivered, my darling, at The Hoo, in Hertfordshire. It grieves me that you had to suffer alone. I've had to rescue families from caves in foreign mountains, when I should be looking after my own family at home. My last postcard, from Siracusa, was written on the very day you were struggling to give life to our second son. I was sick with worry. But, darling Kate, you sound well and happy now. I hope this is true. Keep safe and when you have the strength, please let me know of your plans for moving out of London. I resent every day of this war, yet every day I love you more, Jim

10th October 1943

Today I visited the cathedral in Siracusa; luckily it's undamaged. One day, when the war is a distant memory, we'll all four come and see it together. Just to think, it's been a place of worship for 15 centuries! But a lot of the city's been destroyed by the Fascists; roads, railways, bridges, buildings, all have to be rebuilt. We'll use local labour, if we can get the Sicilians down from the mountains. They'll probably be as unsure which side they're on as the Arabs were. Countless numbers of kisses to you, Jim

3rd January 1944

Dearest Kate, Received a bundle of your letters today. It took a long time for them to reach me. I've been lost in them for hours. Thank heavens you've left London. I'll sleep better knowing you're safe in the Cornish countryside. Sweet dreams my darling. Your ever loving Jim

Ear of Dionysius in 1944

28th May 1944

Dearest Kate
This fascinating grotto is called The Ear of Dionysius. I went into the huge interior, all hewn by human labour in 400 BC, and was amazed. I whispered, Kate, I love you (I was all alone), your name echoed through the grotto and the words came roaring back, magnified a thousand times.
Ever yours, Jim

ITALY

PIONEER ARCHIVES

NOTES ON THE OPERATION OF
CIVIL LABOUR IN ITALY

We followed on the heels of The British 8th Army who led the assault in the south eastern end of Sicily, in the heat of the summer, 1943

The plan now is simple and straightforward. An Italian-speaking officer accompanied by a single NCO proceeds daily up each of the main axes of attack; their job is to enter the town or village, as soon as it falls, button-hole the town mayor and persuade him by any means to coerce each man in the community capable of heavy work – to be ready to assist the Royal Engineers in their task of road construction as soon as tools and equipment can be brought up the line.

The Italian, be he soldier or civilian, does not always take kindly to front-line warfare and he was not just to be had. He was in the hills or anywhere but where he would have been useful for repairing roads under shellfire.

High in the hills, as we advanced, we found gallant little bands of partisans, living in caves and hollows in the rocks and creeping out at night to harry the Germans and find such food as they could to keep themselves alive.

BARI - R. Università Benito Musso

24th June 1944

We landed at Bari last week by plane. The harbour walls are severely damaged from the explosion of an ammunitions ship; you may have heard about it. Even worse, the infra-structure of the city has been decimated. We have to get services working again. This picture shows the Universita Benito Musso and its garden of palm trees in the moonlight, but it no longer exists, it's been totally destroyed. What a dumb-founding waste. I'm so sick of this war. I know I'm lucky, not to be in the front-line – I only have to clear-up afterwards, but I care for none of it. I care only to get back to you. Jim CMF

5th May 1945 Censored

Hitler's killed himself. We've been rushed to Milan. Armistice more chaotic than the ******* war. Impossible amounts of paperwork. Shouldn't complain. Lot safer than **** **** ****** in Sicily. Last night Gen. ***** ******** rewarded us — a free visit to Tosca at La ******** Scala. Didn't mean a thing to me except the heroine's hair was curly like yours and I imagined running my fingers through**** **** *** ******* *** ***** and ******* *** the minute I find you in that Cornish farm cottage where you've been waiting for me for three years. Three years. Yours ever, Jim

FRANCE

PIONEER ARCHIVES

THE GENERAL'S SPEECH

Soldier-workers of the Common Cause! My recent tour amongst you has shown me a race of Men! A race of fine men at work and fully conscious of the Great Cause for which they strive! Men who refused to modify their ancient faith!

I have seen a race of men hard like stones; strong with the strength of bulls; and as courageous as lions! And I say unto you,

FORWARD
ONWARD
TO
VICTORY!

24th September 1945, Dieppe

Kate,
my beloved,
Almost there!
NOTHING,
not this hacking cough, the whole camp is heaving with it, nor the roughest of Channel crossings will dampen my spirits tonight.
It's over.
I'm coming home,
forever,
Jim

PIONEER ARCHIVES

NOTIFICATION OF IMPENDING RELEASE
2915 CIVIL LABOUR UNIT

Pioneer Corps Name: Spencer William Neat
Army No: 13041088   Present Rank: W/SGT
Military Conduct: Good

This NCO has served with this Unit in the capacity of Works Supervisor, supervising the employment of civilian labour in various parts of Italy, Sicily and North Africa. He has shewn himself keen, conscientious and honest at all times. He acquired a working knowledge of the Italian and Arabic languages, enabling him to communicate with the town authorities on the behalf of the unit. I have no hesitation in reporting that his conduct has been exemplary and I fully recommend him in his future applications for employment.

Date: 14 September 1945

Officer's Signature: V.L. Wright, Lt.

Extract from Kate's Diaries

September 1945
Bodmin Moor, Cornwall

In a frock fitted at the waist and flared to just below the knee, I'm pegging out the washing, two pairs of boys' shorts, four grey socks, flapping in the warm September breeze. This world is mine. Mine and my boys'. One's playing at my feet, crawling, pulling up grass and sprinkling it into the washing basket; the other's collecting ants and worms, dropping them in on top.

All this will end. Because Hitler is dead. My hair, wiry and wild, blows across my face so I don't see Jim running over the pitted field towards the cottage, waving his army cap; not till I hear his voice calling my name over and over again. I glance down into the washing basket at the dead grass, the worms, the hungry ants. Small hands grasp at my hem.

Within an hour, Mary is conceived.

FOUND

MARY J. OLIVER'S NOTE BOOK

May 19th 2007

I open my eyes a fraction and, yes – someone is standing close to the bed. Is it Piers wandering around? I'm surreptitiously feeling for his foot, with my own, when an intense red light fills the room and a voice I'd forgotten fills the air, 'Mary, is it you? Have I found you at last? Is it you?' My father! Twenty five years since he died, and he's standing beside my bed, in his prime. As handsome as hell with his crop of yellow hair and his hesitant smile. His way with clothes hasn't changed either – that raincoat, tied at the waist with old binder-twine, the cause of such chagrin in the past, triggers now a flood of tenderness. Will he speak again? Or is that it? I try to fix him like a photo, suspended in bright Rothko silence, disappointed for a moment, when the image dissolves, the darkroom a dark room once more, but then joy – like transfused blood – rushes through my veins.

May 20th 2007

Only now can I see how precarious it was for my parents when my father came back from the war. My mother had coped perfectly well without him, found unimaginable inner strength. A city girl, she'd learned to survive with two baby boys in a remote cottage with no water, no electricity, they'd created a bond beyond words. She and her sons adhered to what they knew like barnacles to granite, had no need of this wild-eyed stranger. Redundant, he alternated between fury and depression, losing forever the power of language. My sudden existence during the severest winter on record couldn't have helped. I must have quadrupled the challenges facing them all. Is it surprising that my brothers, already disturbed by the arrival of a strange man in their lives, resented my demands for nourishment and attention day and night? That my father was out of his depth? My mother unable to bond?

What is surprising is that Dad and I existed on the periphery of this family and, in the bleakness of that landscape, failed to find each other.

Who was he? I bloody need him right now. Childhood stuff keeps coming back.

Bodmin Moor

1946

Someone pokes a finger in my face.
A deep voice tells the finger off
then thanks the driver.
A moorland draught wrinkles
my two square inches of exposed skin
as someone transfers me from the ambulance
to the hood end of a pram
and tucks me in at right angles.
Two boys clamber on board
filling up the remaining space entirely.
The deep voice warns them
to keep their feet to themselves.
A farm gate is clanked open, slammed shut.
I'm pushed for a mile and a half
over thunderous fields.
My eyes mini-universes
not here yet.

Cheeky Blighter

1949

I follow the farmer's wife into a large dimly lit room and see, by the window, a beautiful maidenhair plant streaming over the sides of a gleaming black grand piano.

'You wait in here,' she says, 'while your dad's getting his wages. I'll bring you something to eat.'

On the far side of the room sits old farmer Penhennick, hardly distinguishable from the faux tapestry of his armchair.

I stay rooted to the spot, till his wife returns with a tray, orange squash for me, tea in a cup and saucer for him and biscuits, arranged in a circle on a small matching plate, for us both.

'Come sit on my knee,' he says, patting his fat old lap. I remain rooted to my spot but, quietly, he says it again. Not knowing what else to do, I oblige.

His rough fingers ferret inside my skirt. I climb down from his knee, walk stiffly towards the door and, with my back to him, wait in silence.

I don't mention it till teatime. 'Did he? Cheeky blighter!' says my mother.

But my father leaps up from the table in one explosive movement, chair crashing to the floor behind him, knotted mouth spitting expletives, blue eyes bulging. Within seconds he's on his bike, has disappeared down the lane headed for the farm.

When he returns he's lost his job as chief herdsman. 'And we got to move out,' he says. I'm sent to bed without any milk.

Evil Primrose

1952

I run out the back door, leap over the garden fence into the field, flatten a mole hill.

Climb the Africa Tree, dislodge a crow's nest.

Scramble over a high bank, feel myself slipping, grab at handfuls of wet grass. That's when I see the evil primrose.

Primula Vulgaris with your fifty pale petals where there should be only five and your thrum-eyed yellow gaze hammering home my terror.

It's massive, a freak and it stinks of rotten fruit. Shall I pick it, take it home? Mum and Dad will think it so peculiar, so rare a sight, they'll stop fighting.

But I'm scared of its huge face, its hairy leaves like dragons' tongues, too scared to snap its monster stem, frightened I'd be strangled by its poisonous threads.

Primula Vulgaris with your fifty pale petals where there should be only five and your thrum-eyed yellow gaze hammering home my terror.

Sister?

1954

From my bedroom, I hear Mum's piercing whisper,

'Staring into the fire all evening, you're in another world. It's that woman you married in Canada. And her baby. Isn't it? Still dreaming about them, after all this time, it's ridiculous. That's what it is, though. Isn't it? Admit it!'

'You don't understand. What I told you back then wasn't entirely true. I wanted you to feel sorry for me, Kate. Jesus Christ, I loved you. I wanted you to marry me.'

'You mean you lied about her?'

'I lied about marrying her, she wasn't my wife.'

'... hmmf ... that doesn't alter the fact that you still spend your time thinking about her, does it?'

'I couldn't bear for you to think of the child as illegitimate ... I like to think of her as Mary's sister.'

'What a shady character you are. How can I believe a word you say?'

Does that mean I've got a sister? And no one told me? Sister? I could do with a sister. Bet she could do with me, too.

The back door slams shut. Dad's leaving. Again. I look out my bedroom window. He's walking away, his small canvas rucksack, that slight limp.

Corps 216 ~~boy~~ Pioneer corps

PARTICULARS of Marriages and Births to be forwarded to the Officer i/c Records for insertion in the soldier's attestation.

No.* 13041083 W/S/Cpl. Neat, Spencer James.

PIONEER CORPS RECORDS

30 APR 1941

* Here insert Army Number, Rank, and Names at full length.

MARRIAGE.

Nationality† of the Soldier ... ...
(specifying whether Bachelor or Widower)

English ~~Bachelor~~ Widower.

Christian Name, Surname and Nationality at Birth† of the Woman ... ...
(specifying whether Spinster or Widow)

Muriel Kate Thomas.
English Spinster.

Place of marriage, specifying Parish, County, &c. ...

St. Peter's Parish Church Marlborough Wilts.

Date of marriage ... ...

12ᵗʰ April 1941.

Names of witnesses who signed the Register ...

M. J. Thomas.
Ernest W. Boot.

Name of the Officiating Minister ~~or Registrar~~ by whom the marriage was recorded ... ...

Alfred J. E. Neads (curate)

† English, Scotch, Irish, &c., &c., as the case may be.

The birth of each child should be reported to the Officer i/c Records (through the Regimental Paymaster) on the reverse side of this form by Officers Commanding Units, immediately on receipt of the information as to the birth.

(10254) Wt.30814/882 300,000 10/40 A.& E.W.Ltd. Gp.695 Forms/A22/57

[P.T.O.

Bachelor or Widower?

A Vixen Screams

1955

My brothers and I hear the cry of an animal. We climb through a barbed wire fence, scramble down the gully, find a creature so young we can't be sure what it is. We take it home.

I feed it milk from my fountain pen. It seems to love me and its nose is sharp. It screeches and its tail is red.

'That's definitely a little vixen,' my Dad says. 'I love her and she's mine,' I bark. In the copse I teach her to sit, to come when called and not to bite.

In the distance a hunting horn; I throw myself on top of her; horses' hooves shake the earth. Creeping home round the dark edge of the field, Little Vixen wrapped up so tight in my cardigan she can hardly breathe.

'She'll have to go, she's getting too big,' Dad says. Mum agrees, 'And she's beginning to smell.'

I carry Little Vixen upstairs to bed, same as I always do. In the morning, she follows me downstairs, same as always. On the kitchen floor, a crate, *Paignton Zoo* painted in red on the side. She's going to travel in a guard's van, alone.

On the way to the station, Little Vixen sticks her wet nose through the bars of the crate and bites my finger.

If I'd Gone to Folkestone

1956

The atmosphere stinks of put-out fires. I never get used to it.
'Come in here,' my dad says, leading me into the sitting room.
It's February; last night's ashes still in the grate. I'm shivering
on the sofa.

'I'm going away for a while, to stay with Queenie, in Folkestone.
You can come too, if you like. She lives by the sea, has a
daughter, Sally, your age, a cousin you've never met. What do
you think? We'll go by train. Get away from here.'

I hear Mum in the hall, 'Where's Mary?' The door bursts open.
'What are you two doing? What's he been saying?'

'He asked me to go away with him, to see my cousin I've never
met.'

'You go on upstairs this minute.' From under my blanket I hear
the fight continue into the night.

A Lean and Wiry Man

1956

April
Dad comes back from the shippon stinking of manure, he's shaving at the kitchen sink stripped to the waist, torn pieces of bloodied cigarette papers stuck to the cuts on his neck.

They're shouting. I'm begging them to stop.

After dark, all their love letters burn in the garden. Who struck the match? He disappears. Some local boys find him unconscious in a ditch, bring him back late, 'lads I taught to read for heaven's sake,' Mum says. They carry him through the house, arrange him carefully in his armchair.

We go to bed. In the morning he's in the same position. Can't tell if he's breathing or not. Mum and I cross the playground, go to school as usual. The school secretary, 'a frightfully just-so little madam', calls the ambulance.

May
The psychiatrist says he was very close to death. Alcohol, which he's not used to, and an overdose of anti-depressants and valium pumped out of his stomach. But she expects him to make a good recovery because of his physique. She calls him 'a lean and wiry man.'

June
Dad's been in hospital for months. We never visit. I don't even know how to get to Bodmin.

July
The psychiatrist rings to tell Mum that he discharged himself this morning and asks if he's turned up here. He hasn't. We don't know where he is. I don't know when I'll see him again.

Pawn

1958

The pretty pieces appeal to me — Dad
demonstrates the moves — a novel
opening gambit — strategy and logic
— how to fight — how to annihilate —
I like it straightaway — see he's
pleased — I feel proud — he teaches
me fool's mate — never be caught out
— castle early — be prepared —
bishops work in tandem — never act
alone — knights jump from behind —
surprise your foe — throw a timely
punch — use your mighty queen —
protect the king — the weakest piece –
with all your strength — but remember
— only the pawn — your smallest
piece can be promoted — and
guarantee victory

Bicep to Bicep

1968

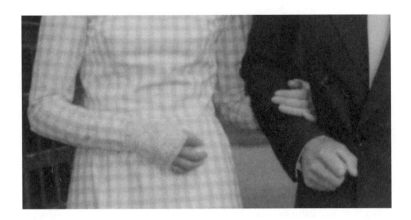

It was his job
to give me away

Yet I wasn't his to give

He never kissed me goodnight
never held my hand
never met me from school
never boiled me an egg

Yet we played chess

Tactics sorted
we head for the altar
bicep to bicep
fists gently furled

NOTE BOOK (cont.)

July 2007

I hatch a plan. To solve this enigma of my father. His absence in the past. His sudden presence in my life now. I'll ask my mother if she has any old papers of his stashed away.

And what about that half-sister who was mentioned just once? Maybe, if she's alive, I'll find her too.

FOUND DOCUMENTS

Letter from Jim to Adam

January 1949

My dear Adam

I write to thank you and Philomena for the parcel – it arrived on Christmas Eve. You can imagine how the children fell upon the biscuits!

Kate says to tell you how she appreciated the tinned peaches, white sugar and flour. We're particularly thankful for the cigarettes. I'd just lost my job on the farm, so your gift was timely indeed. I work at the brick factory now, grim and filthy it is too; brings in 3 pounds a week – and a whole load of red dust that seeps into every corner of the house.

Kate starts teaching next week. I wish she didn't have to, but since I can't provide enough for the family, I have to accept it. At the age of 29, she's learnt to ride a bike to get her to the school, two miles away. She'll have to take Mary with her, on the back.

Good news that the crops in Eldon thrive! I can see you both so clearly in my mind's eye, milking the cows and cutting the corn, though I guess you're snowed under right now.

My country is taking longer than yours to get back on its feet after the war. Now that you're rid of Prime Minister Bennett, it seems you're being treated with respect at last. Here the ruling class still views the country as if it were a romantic landscape painting, you know, a fox hunt with the odd peasant in the background.

Funnily enough, my young niece, Lola, fed up with this country, has just emigrated to Canada. Hope she fares better than I did.

Your old friend,
Jim

Letter from Jim to Frank*

February 16th 1970

I think of you often, Frank, though it's sixteen years since your last letter. My letters to you remain unanswered. Perhaps you've moved from Chaplain Terrace.

This is to let you know that Kate and I are travelling to Canada, to visit our eldest son who has emigrated to Montreal. Another family member drawn there. He'll do well, being somewhat more qualified than I was! Kate's eager to see the grand-daughters. We've flights booked for April 24th.

It's thirty-four years since you paid for my deportation and I sailed back to England aboard the White Star Ausonia.

As a young man I made many difficult journeys across Canada clinging to the underside of boxcars, as you know. This time I shall travel in relative style. Even if I don't hear from you before April, I'm going to get a train to Toronto and do my utmost to track you down. I believe you're fifteen years older than me; that makes you a mere eighty-one.

I look forward to finding you and to that familiar journey alongside Lake Ontario.

Yours Jim

* Frank Schofield left Canada in 1955, returning to Korea to teach at Seoul National University. He died there in 1970, about the time Jim was looking for him in Toronto. He was buried in the Korean National Cemetery, Seoul, the first foreigner to be so honoured.

Exchange between Jim and Marcia Williams, Secretary to Harold Wilson

1980

Dear Marcia Williams

As a life-long supporter of the Labour movement, I would be grateful if you would convey my sympathies to Harold Wilson on his urgent admittance to hospital in Penzance last night. I and my fellow supporters sincerely hope it is not a recurrence of his colon cancer and send him our best wishes for a speedy recovery, so that he can continue his journey to the Scillies.

I live, with my wife, in nearby Newlyn. We have a small spare bedroom and would be only too happy to provide a quiet place for him and his wife to stay before continuing their journey, should they need it.

All best wishes,

Jim Neat

HOUSE OF COMMONS
LONDON SWIA OAA
20th June 1980.

Dear Mr. Neat,

Sir Harold has asked me to thank
you for your letter to him in hospital.
He is sorry not to be able to reply
personally but unfortunately he is not
yet able to deal with his correspondence,
as I am sure you will appreciate.

Nevertheless, he wanted you to
know he had seen your letter and how much
he appreciated all you said. He also particularly
asked me to send his warm good wishes to you
and to tell you he will keep in mind your kind
invitation.

With good wishes,

Yours sincerely,

M. Williams

Private Secretary.

Mr. S.J. Neat.

Alas for Mrs Hickman*

Undated

A bare-knuckle fight, Bill Neat (The Bristol Butcher) v
Tom Hickman (Gas Man), on Hungerford Common, was
recorded by William Hazlitt in the New Monthly
Magazine, 1821

Come noon, I lumbers into the ring & quietly I disrobes. I has
to wait, till Gas Man struts out onto the grassy knoll, sucking
at his orange with supercilious air. He tosses the peel at the
chanting crowd, booms, 'So! You're Bill Neat, The Bristol
Butcher. I'll knock more blood out of thy great carcase than
thou ever knocked out of a bullock's!'

Straightway I head-fakes him to the left, but gets a liver shot in
the right. I'm down, a lifeless lump of lard & gristle. Is that it,
finished, in the first bleeding round?

I thinks on the wife, the shame of it & I'm up on me feet, me
arms like sledge-hammers. I holds him in a clinch,
rabbit-punching the back of his skull, till he sinks; blood drains
from his ugly mug, out his eyes, out his nose, out his ears.

But he heaves himself up & smiles his ghastly smile.

Eighteen rounds later, his brow screwed up against the setting
sun, he falls for the last time.

I stoops & limply shakes his broken fist – the sign for my homing
pigeon to take to the skies & fly to the bosom of my beloved
wife – the message, Alas for Mrs Hickman! attached to its little
pink leg.

---

* A poem in my father's hand-writing, inspired by Hazlitt's article, The Fight.

Bill Neat, The Bristol Butcher, engraving by Percy Roberts

Exchange between my father and me

September 1982

Dear Mary

Mary, I so love that name. You probably know that Kate chose the boys' names. But your name, she said, was up to me. I've never told you why I chose Mary, but now I will.

As you know, I lived in Canada for many years, before Mum and I met. And very turbulent years they were. I was ashamed of them and Kate doesn't let me talk about them anyway, so please don't mention this to her.

During that time, I was in love with a Ukrainian girl. When she died in childbirth, I went to pieces. However, I don't want to linger on that; I prefer to remember our daughter, who survived. She was adopted but, because I was legally branded a vagrant, I wasn't allowed to see her. We'd planned to call her Mariya, after her grandmother, meaning Beloved Star of the Sea. Naming you after her was my way of surviving without her. This hasn't diminished the love I've felt for you. I feel in you I've loved you both, but it's been a love I haven't known how to show.

I'm sure that's hard for you to believe or understand. I could see your isolation in the family but I was isolated myself and lacked the knowledge, the guts, to reach out to you.

I hope you one day find a way to forgive me.

I'm so proud to hear about your Glasgow exhibition, wish I could come to the opening. Please send a photo. I'm enjoying my bees and getting on quite well at my art class too. Am sending you two drawings; one of School House from the playground. The other is Gwavas Quay in Newlyn. What do you think? Any talent to speak of?

Love to your dear girls, I enclose £1 each for them.

Your ever loving Dad

Dear Dad

Thank you for the drawings. I really like them, they're lively and intensely observed. Nice memories to have of the places where we've lived. The only thing I'd suggest is that you don't add charcoal to your pencil drawings. For the darkest areas, just use a softer pencil.

Girls will be writing to you soon,
love
Mary

School House from the playground

Gwavas Quay, Newlyn

To Kate, From Jim, 1981, graphite drawing from Camille Pissarro's
painting of Norwood (my boyhood home) painted circa 1863

Queenie's First and Last Letter to Kate
13 Kingsnorth Gardens, Folkestone, Kent

10th September 1983

Dear Kate

No, no, what dreadful news. But thank you for your letter enclosing Jim's drawing, I shall have it framed.

Little did I know when I said goodbye to him in the early part of the year, that I'd never see him again, when he kissed me goodbye, he held himself very straight, he seemed to have a young look in his eyes, which took me back many years, I can't believe he's gone.

Of all his women, I am of course the one who knew him best, the only one who knew him all his life.

I've unearthed all sorts of things for you, a poem in a hand I don't recognise that must go back to that first voyage when he jumped ship in Cape Town – newspaper cuttings from the time he spent in Australia – a rather suspect, illegible diary from Canada. He asked me to look after them all when he married you, I have no need of them now.

So Kate dear, I will close, you know your family are welcome to stay with David and I, if ever they are in Folkestone, yours in grief, he was my best and oldest friend,

Queenie

Document Enclosed in Queenie's Letter

Bliss in Cape Town, 1921

I done find Jim in dockyard lyin on shed floor. He look scare, I close door gentle. 'No worry,' I say, 'I call Bliss,' an I kiss him rose flower mouth.

Pleasure sailor that my job, but this diffrent. I only fourteen, don forget, he fifteen, sixteen most. Old sailor done rape him cabin boy every day, Jim tell me, so he jump ship. 'I like you yellow hair,' I say.

I bring him string beans an a pear from my step-daddy plot, cassava an rice from ship I work nights, a mango, a plum an a small pickle fish one day.

He love Table Mountain peek upside lil window wile we eat an laugh lot, roll round. 'Oh Bliss!' he say, 'Marry me, then you not do this nice thing with bad men you not love – never gain.'

'You mad sugarbush, No!' I say an throw him white arm far way. 'You desert ship, you got no right, no pass. Law here hang you. Liberty Belle she in dock an I know she sail tonight. You go.'

Soon as dark Jim an me we go quiet from shed we lay. Crew on waterfront all busy, all girls an boys they say bye-bye.

Jim he fly like mosquito round me, here, there, he kiss me. Then short time hush, him sweet head in Bliss black hands. Up, up gang plank he zig zag. Gone.

Document Enclosed in Queenie's Letter

Western Australian, Thursday 5th July 1922
Stowaway Imprisoned
Action by Uglymen Secures Release

A penniless young man, James William Neat, native of London, was last week imprisoned in Fremantle Jail, charged with having stowed away on the S.S. Liberty Belle, which arrived in Fremantle on Monday.

Neat, who had previously been employed on the S.S. Albany, left the United Kingdom, intending to emigrate to Australia. But when the boat docked to refuel in Cape Town, he went missing due to unknown circumstances. Two weeks later he stowed away on the S.S. Liberty Belle and completed his journey.

The Captain reported him to the authorities on arrival in WA, but vouched for him, saying that after the lad gave himself up half-way across the Indian Ocean, he worked harder than anyone on board, and declared he would be more than happy to employ him.

Neat, however, intent on helping us to build our new country, insisted on staying in Fremantle.

A mandatory fine of £6 was imposed. Unable to pay, he was given a prison sentence of unspecified duration.

When the Uglyman's Association heard of his case, they made a successful representation to the Minister for Justice. Vice-President, Mr Mann, stated, '*when we can get a man who has courage enough to come over here without a penny, to make another start in life, there is not much good in putting him in gaol and then throwing him out amongst the unemployed. This young man is as fine a type as we could wish for. He can be usefully employed by our Association and we will set him on his feet.*'

Neat was immediately released and is now employed building bungalows on the outskirts of our town for bereaved widows of the Great War.

Document Enclosed in Queenie's Letter

Western Australian
Thursday 6th September 1922

Exploding Horse

Police are looking for an immigrant worker and the daughter of a farmer from the Darling Scarp area. It is reported that while the farmer was at market, the couple left a gate open, while supposedly 'working' together in a field of fresh clover. Distracted from their duties, they failed to notice that the farmer's valuable cart-horse had entered the field, at least not until the beast exploded from a surfeit of gas.

It appears that they attempted to burn and bury the carcase, and left a note for the farmer on the kitchen table: *Horse thieves stole Stanley; we're out looking for him; supper's in the oven.*

The farmer discovered his half-burnt, half-buried beast the following day. He is offering an award of £25 for the capture of his daughter and a larger award for that of the immigrant worker. They were last seen hitch-hiking with their arms around each other on the coast road to Perth.

Document Enclosed in Queenie's Letter

Daily News (Perth WA)
Monday 14 January 1923

GETTING WORSE
USE OF OBSCENE LANGUAGE.

YOUNG MEN HEAVILY FINED.

His occupation of the Police Court Bench in recent months has convinced the P.M. (Mr. A. B. Kidson) that the use of obscene language in the city and suburbs is increasing daily, and he has set out, determinedly, to wipe out the evil. Last week he announced from the Bench his intention to severely punish offenders, and he put his words into effect this morning.

Three young men, Charles Marias (26), clerk, Richard Sonnon (24), miner, and Spencer Neat (19), miner, paid a visit to Crawley Baths on Saturday. It was their intention to have a bathe, but they indulged in too much liquor before leaving the city. Seeing their condition, the superintendent refused them admission. Immediately Marias and Neat showed their resentment by using foul language, while Sonnon made himself offensive by committing a nuisance alongside the bathing sheds. Constable Bannear then came on the scene and arrested the three. The language, according to the constable, was vile, Neat who gave him considerable trouble, being the worst offender.

This morning at the City Court, the P.M., after having expressed his determination to heavily penalise this class of offence, fined Neat £6, and Marias and Sonnon £5 each.

NOTE BOOK (cont.)

September 2007

These findings give rise to more dreams. More memories, more research and a determination to ensure that at least one hobo's life does not go unrecorded.

His Outhouse

A queen excluder. Two boxes of beeswax. Stained frames stacked haphazardly in a corner. Matches, dead on the ground. A dozen sterile 1lb jars, their screw tops coated with grime. The smoker still stinking of creosote. Corrugated cardboard religiously shredded. His veiled bee hat with the odd rip in it. Hanging from a spike behind the door, the zip-up dungarees he'd been issued by the school where he was employed as janitor. The binder-twine he tied around his waspish waist (the chagrin of that binder-twine). Half a twisted packet of Polos. A tea caddy labelled *GLUE & FUSES* in his fiercely sloping hand. Withwind growing in and out of the warped roof. While the keeper of bees himself – stretched out on a tight white sheet, belly lavishly knotted with sutures, a nurse morphining his pain away, wiping down his yellow skin, loving him more than we knew how – is still asking after his bees; *They like trees, and freedom,* he says. *On a warm afternoon, let them swarm.*

December 2007

His Hands Froze

riding the rails, the skin split
and his nails turned black.

A boy without wings leapt out of those hands,
fell to the ground, loped off – lost to the night.

His Saskatchewan lover died in a drought, their prairie daughter
lost to locusts.

Years later I hear in the dust
my sister call.

3rd January 2008

I've tracked down Queenie's second daughter, Sally, 'the cousin I never met'. Still living in Folkestone, she's keen to meet up.

She never throws anything away! Boxes of evidence are dragged out of her spare room and we spend a weekend sorting them. 'Take what you need,' she says. 'And you should go visit Lola. She took loads of stuff when Queenie died.' She gives me Lola's address in Ontario, where she's lived since 1946.

18th January 2008

With Lola's first reply I realize I've struck gold: 'I've a ferocious appetite for genealogy / have cracked ancestor.com. Will send you everything I've got on Jim.'

A package arrives. Letters and photographs. Passenger Lists. Prison Records. Hospital Notes. Deportation Orders. Call-Up Papers.

In my hands I have documents I never dreamed existed.

5th February 2008

I receive this letter from Serge Malinski, Saskatchewan Hospital, North Battleford

Dear Mary

 I am afraid I won't be able to meet with you to answer your questions. It's years since I even left my room. I'm a mute, you see. But my memory is excellent and I'm happy to tell you what I know in writing.

 The whole of Saskatchewan had been stripped bare by the drought in June 1936. Ma and Pa, distraught by the collapse of their business, had gone east looking for work, leaving our step-sister, Lizbietta, to look after me and Zenaida, my little sister. She was like a mom to us.

 I remember it was an enjoyable few weeks. She found a stack of comics in a neighbour's barn and we spent one whole weekend gluing Buck Rogers to our bedroom ceiling and Tarzan all over the walls. It was the funniest thing we'd done in ages.

 On the Monday, we walked home after school, a hot wind blowing fine black topsoil in all directions, like thick smoke. From the gate, I could see the back door flapping and banging on its hinges. As we got nearer, a clacking sound fill the air, not the radio, not Lizbietta singing to herself, clattering around in the kitchen. This was the deep low-pitched clacking buzz we dreaded. I ran indoors.

 The kitchen was thick with locusts gorging on remnants of porridge stuck to the saucepan, sucking the grease off the top of the stove, fighting over a pile of potato skins in the sink. The floor was covered with them, dead and dying.

 I pushed Zenaida into the front parlour. Shouted at her if she didn't stop snivelling I'd wallop her, slammed the door shut in her face.

 Ran upstairs, could hear wheezing inside my chest, bodies crunching under my feet. On the landing I called out, Liz, you up here? No answer, but above the vibrating hum all around me, I heard a faint mewing sound, like a baby's cry. I knew Liz's baby was due soon. But not yet.

Liz? Lizbietta? I flung open her bedroom door. Liz's room, which always smelt of talcum powder, Liz's room where she wrote in her journal every evening after tea, where every morning she gently smoothed the patchwork bedcover her Ukrainian grandmother had given her, where she wrote to Jim when Jim was away, where she always put a jam jar of prairie flowers next to her bed when she knew he was likely to visit.

A metallic, feral smell hit me. A pool on the floor. A crawling heap on the bed. Wings vibrating on the patchwork quilt. On Lizbietta. Everything dark with dust from the fields. A small limb quivered.

I remember walking backwards out of the room. Went downstairs. Sat on the settee beside Zenaida. Just sat staring at the framed photo of Lizbietta's friend, Norman Falkner, which hung above the fireplace. Grabbed hold of Zenaida, started running the length of Queen Street, dragging her along behind me.

How long can a baby live without milk? I was coughing up phlegm, could hardly breathe. Zenaida screaming at me to stop.

Must have taken us twenty minutes to reach Norman's house, the only person I knew who had a phone. 'Liz's baby,' I whispered and threw up on the doorstep. 'Holy shit.' He called the doctor. Made us a drink from Saskatoon berries he said he'd picked from the side of the railroad that morning. 'You kids,' he said, 'you better stay here tonight.'

Zenaida fell asleep on the sofa. Every so often she made gulping noises, like she was still crying. 'How about you, Serge?' Norman asked me, 'You going to be okay?' I couldn't speak. No words would come. Not after finding Lizbietta like that.

Next day Norman told Miss McKinley, my teacher, what had happened, that I couldn't speak. She notified the school board for professional advice. Her intention must have been misinterpreted, because a Governor arrived the same day and told her that he couldn't afford to support kids who didn't cooperate with policy.

And therefore in accordance with some rule in the 1931 Education Act, I was removed and sent that day to an institution deemed more suitable

I thank you for getting in touch. I'm afraid I know nothing of the child born an orphan. Your half-sister. Those times were so wretchedly bad, I lost all contact with family. I do know though that Norman lived to a good age. He was one of Canada's celebrities for a while but shamefully was allowed to die in poverty. It's been helpful putting this into words and I'm relieved to hear that Jim survived his hobo days, made a new life for himself back home.

Sincerely,
Serge Malinski

Enclosures:

Norman Falkner, 1894-1984, the world's best,
and Saskatoon's only, one-legged ice-skater

March 2008

Before Mum Dies She Falls in Love Again

with Dad.
My obsession to follow his hobnail boots across Canada
breathes new life into her fluid-filled lungs
awakes in her a moth-eaten madness
an appetite to upturn stones
and my insistence on the existence of my half sister
is oxygen to her old heart.
'Hope you find her,' she whispers.
She even pays my fare.

April 2008

Before Dark

Struggling to sleep, strangely alert, I sense my father standing by my bed. Again. Not alone this time. A tall woman with brown tangled hair, in a cotton frock of no colour at all, leaning into him. 'Lizbietta,' he says, with unbridled pride. She steps forward, 'Mary,' she says, 'it wouldn't have been right to visit before – but now's the time – we've a small crack of light – come with us – let's find your sister – come.' And, gently upending, we Chagall round the room uncannily drawn to the rising moon.

MARY J. OLIVER'S CANADA DIARY

2nd May, 2008

Ramada Hotel, Gatwick
I'm crossing Canada. (Good grief.)

4 – 9th May

Vancouver Island

Remains of ancient forest, British Columbia, felled in the 1920s

9 – 16th May

Edmonton, Alberta

Clocks go back an hour.
I step down from the train's massive height
at this surprisingly small station.
Walk the ridiculous length of the platform.
Adam's son is waiting for me.
Drives me to a Ukrainian Heritage Centre.
I'm not sure he believes my story but no one could be kinder.
A hot wind blows.
The horizon's curved. I'm on top of the world.
Shoulders burning.
Onto to the Shiloh Church
all that remains of the African pioneer community.
The white cross where Adam lies.
The spot where the sod-house stood.
Just soft Prairie loam now.

Shiloh Cemetery 2008

16th May

North Battleford, Saskatchewan

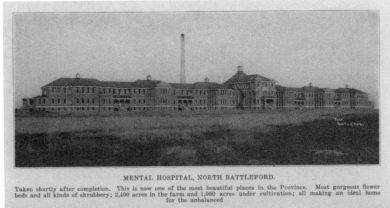

MENTAL HOSPITAL, NORTH BATTLEFORD.

Taken shortly after completion. This is now one of the most beautiful places in the Province. Most gorgeous flower beds and all kinds of shrubbery; 2,400 acres in the farm and 1,000 acres under cultivation; all making an ideal home for the unbalanced

Greyhound bus stops right outside the hospital.

17th – 22nd May

Saskatoon

600 Queen Street today

Clocks go back another hour.
I arrive late evening.
Air balmy, warm as blood.
This is it. I know it. Saskatoon, the city where they met.
Where it happened.
I find my way to 600 Queen Street,
check in at Valentyna's board and lodgings,
now called Aunt Aggie's Guest House.
Cross the river over University Bridge,
explore the campus as the sun goes down.
Next morning walk on down to The Bethany Home
at the far end of the street.
Stand on the steps he was pushed down.
Sorry, says a member of staff,
all records were destroyed in 1952.

I dream of my sister walking out of the Home
bare-foot down the steps
in an orange bridal gown, laughing.

Bethany Home for Unwed Mothers, 802 Queen Street, Saskatoon

Demolished February 2018

As we rush towards each other, smoke billows
from the doorway, engulfing her.

22nd May

Fly from Saskatoon to Toronto

over the haunted remains of Whitby Hospital, closed 1995,
demolished 2005

over Mrs MacTaggart's library

over Toronto Gaol, closed in the 1970s

now a tourist attraction:
'door on left leads to execution drop area,
cells on right held those awaiting execution'.

24th May
On to Ottawa

Clocks go back an hour. Again. I can't believe how vast this country is.

Taxi drops me off at midnight. Lola rushes into the street. I'm meeting my first cousin, Queenie's first-born, Jim's favourite niece for whom he stole chocolate when she was six months old. Meeting her for the first time.

We hug each other in the tree-lined avenue, the warmth of the day still rising from the pavement. She's 84. Was five foot two in her prime, now she's four foot ten, wears a short dark wig and copper eye shadow. Speaks the King's English, the fashion when she sailed from Southampton to Toronto in 1948, 'There's only one Canadian accent' she tells me, 'I like to be different.'

Lola, 2008

'You're like your father, angular,' she says, eyeing me mischievously, 'not curvaceous and pretty like his sisters and me. It helps to be plump.' She pats her face, 'But I really do need laser treatment on my left jowl; I sleep on that side so it's not as taut as I'd like. What I really want is a tummy tuck.' 'But you're a lovely shape,' I say. 'Yes, but naked I'm yuck.'

We reach the end of the hallway and enter her kitchen. There's a letter on the table, in childish handwriting. 'It's from my mother to my father, on leaving him,' she says, 'Read it.'

Dear Terry, feel kind towards your little girl, I never do anything real wrong, I'm just full of romance and I can't help that, darling, lots of folk feel romantic, only romance never comes their way. Romance, adventure, everything that speaks of youth and things that make life worth living always come my way and tempt me from paths of convention. This letter comes from a girl who longs for winds as warm as winds of summer south. I could never be a suburban cabbage. Lots and lots of love and kisses, your little girl, Queenie.

Lola's dad, she tells me, was a professional boxer, raised her and they adored each other; they explored London together, collecting discarded fruit from under the market stalls, on Saturday nights they watched the dogs chase the electric hare race round the track at White City, Sundays he'd dress her up in her Sunday best to visit the British Museum.

'When war broke I discovered it was a great time to be young and single. London was flooded with troops, it was all dates and dinners and dancing.'

Lola, 1939

'And afterwards it was so boring, I had to escape. It's in the blood. I found it in me to leave Dad and sailed from Southampton on a grey morning in January, 1948. Destination Toronto. I was twenty two.'*

I thought I was tired. But I'm riveted by what she's telling me about her early years in Canada, finding work modelling in art schools while trying to establish her reputation as a writer. She hitch-hiked across the Trans-Canada Highway before it was paved. She didn't have a map, 'no idea where the mountains were, or even in what order the provinces came.'

* I could never quite make Queenie's or Lola's dates add up...

She submitted scripts based on her travels to the CBC, met a handsome young newsreader, married him.

'Personally I never minded being a sex object,' she tells me, 'After all, that's how I regarded a man. I just didn't want to wait on him. I'm continuously amazed how some women wash, water and feed the brute.

'Not that we were sexually compatible in the slightest,' she adds, 'but we shared left wing views – and it got me my job in photo-journalism.'

Lola shows me to my room, her late-husband's study, walls lined with left-wing political treatises and a stunning collection of photographs by Tina Modotti. I fall on *Diary of a Super Tramp, Confessions of an Immigrant Daughter, As For Me and My House, The Lost Ten Years, The Great Depression, Deemed Unsuitable**. I cannot sleep for reading.

In the morning she says, 'Keep them, he'd love to think people are still studying this stuff.'

After a walk with her old dog, we lie together on her late husband's day-bed, exhausted after our late night, and drift off to sleep in the sunshine that's pouring through the window.

We wake up, and it's almost dark. She opens a bottle of wine. 'Do you know that Jim got clipped round the ear by a constable for stealing chocolate for you when you were a baby?' I ask her. She laughs, No, she's never heard that one. But she does remember meeting him when she was a teenager, soon after he returned to England from Canada. 'It was his intrepid jaunts that triggered

* By William Henry Davies, Laura Goodman Salverson, Sinclair Ross, Barry Broadfoot, Pierre Berton, R. Bruce Shephard

mine. I fell in love with his hare-brained stories from around the world. But then, I was always falling in love,' she says, and spent the rest of the evening giving me one hilarious example after another.

'And now we're falling in love!' The unanticipated comradeship is intoxicating. And ridiculous. Discussing everything under the moon. Sisters giggling into the night.

FINAL ENTRY

June 2018

My Sister's Brilliant Idea

The quarter-moon is smiling in the Cornish sky.
'Just think,' it says, out the corner of its mouth,
'I'm the same moon that your sister drooled over
all those years ago in Saskatoon.'
This annoys me – I've turned the world
half upside down looking for her.
        'Yes, the same moon that lit-up
          the grass-hoppers that invaded the city
       the night she was born,
          the same moon that illuminated the dust that hung
        over her as she waited
      to learn who she was,
       the same moon that startles her profile
      the evening she dies –
       before orbiting on without her.
      Yet no one has a bad word to say about you,
        "Look at the moon!" they say, "Isn't it beautiful?"
       Of course you're beautiful.
        Night or day, fat or thin, white or red
          unattainable, you're always bloody beautiful.'
'Oh, shut up you two.'
I hear a laid-back Canadian accent,
way beyond the moon. 'Give it a break,
can't you see? Unreachable? Unbeautiful?
Beautiful.'

'IN COURT'

DEFENDANT
Jim Neat, a young man

WITNESSES (in order of appearance)
D. R Fletcher, Superintentant, Whitby Hospital, Ontario
Queenie, Jim's youngest sister
Mrs J. MacTaggart, Therapist, Whitby Hospital
Lizbietta, Jim's lover or wife
Valentyna and Viktor, Lizbietta's adoptive parents
Adam, Jim's friend, Afro-Canadian pioneer farmer
Professor Frank Schofield, patient, Whitby Hospital
Alice Schofield, Schofield's wife
Daphne Fletcher, Fletcher's wife
V. L. Wright. Lt., British Army
Kate, Jim's wife
Mary, Jim's daughter
Marcia Williams, Harold Wilson's secretary
Bill Neat, the Bristol Butcher, Jim's ancestor
Bliss, Cape Town sex worker
Western Australian, newspaper reporter
Daily News (Perth W.A.), newspaper reporter
Sally, Queenie's second daughter
Serge Malinski, Lizbietta's step-brother
Norman Falkner, one-legged ice-skater of Saskatoon
Lola, Queenie's first daughter

VERDICT

Remember that what you are told is really threefold:
shaped by the teller,
reshaped by the listener,
concealed from both by the dead man of the tale.

Vladamir Nabokov
The Real Life of Sebastian Knight

AUTHOR'S NOTE

My father seldom spoke about the years he spent in Canada before he met my mother. A mysterious presence in our lives, always on the periphery of the family, he seldom spoke at all.

His death in 1983 seemed a relatively insignificant event and I got on with my life. I was active in the art world and busy bringing up my two girls. I almost forgot about him, until in 2006 events caused me to wonder for the first time, who in heaven's name was he?

This long narrative poem, as I see it, is a distillation of ten years of research into his astonishing history. In my attempt to give him life, where I found gaps in his narrative I have often augmented tantalizing fragments of information with imagined details. In order to keep his story concise and spare, I simplified when necessary and merged some events. Some names have been changed where the narrative demanded it, and while many of the characters existed – as evidenced by the documents included – there are a few invented figures who help move the story forward.

It is not the whole truth. But what is? My intention has been to make a small work of art out of an ordinary man's extraordinary life.

ACKNOWLEDGEMENTS

Grateful acknowledgement to the editors of the following publications in which versions of some of these poems have appeared: *The Naugatuck River Review* (USA), *Compas* (University of Oxford), SPM Publishing (London), *Defining Moments* (Global Words Press), *PLUME* (USA), *The New Welsh Reader* (volume 15), *The Fenland Reed* (Issue 5), And *Other Poems, Hysteria* (volume 4 and 5), *Bridgewatcher & Other Poems, South 53, From Hallows to Harvest* (Cinnamon Press).

I would like to thank tutors, family and friends: David Stouck, Penelope Shuttle, Katrina Naomi, Alessandra Ausenda, Alice Kavounas, Alyson Hallet, Fiona Benson, Lynne Hjelmgaard, Gayle Ashton, Nancy Mattson, Helen Richards, Deborah Came, Dorothy Degenhardt, Salma Saddique, all members of Penzance Stanza Group, John Allford, Miranda Cox, Matthew Dennis, Christopher Neat, Timothy Neat, Steve Tanner, Miki Ashford, Chris Morley, Robbie Smith, Leander Lane, Tony McIntyre, Pamela MacRae (Lola), Sally Ivory, Jolanda Klein, Birgitta Lundmark, Lucy Anderson, Marlene Kaspar.

I thank Piers from the bottom of my heart; also my precious progeny, Polly, Tommy and Peter; Clare, Lena and Becca and my extended family, Des, Steph, Maya and Max, Emma, Andy, Mae and Eddie, Charles, Christine and Finlay.

I am grateful to Whitby Archive for the supply of photographic material on pages 39, 54, 57 and 67.

ABOUT THE AUTHOR

Mary J. Oliver is an artist and writer. In 2017, the original manuscript of *Jim Neat* was awarded 2nd prize by New Welsh Writing – Memoir. Five of the poems from it have been set to music for piano and voice by the composer Judith Bailey. Oliver's poems have appeared in many periodicals and anthologies in UK and US. Competition awards include those judged by Paul Muldoon and Ruth Padel. She is editor of *Piccolina*, a poetry newsletter promoting live-poetry events in Cornwall, UK and her current project involves integrating poetry and gouache painting.